Praise for

An Angel at My Door

Empowering, inspiring and visionary – Jo Lynam's *An Angel at My Door* takes you on an extraordinary journey that gives life to ideas you never thought were possible. She shows you that an unwavering vision and commitment to a "good life" can lead to powerful roles you may have never considered for someone with disability. This perspective might just make a difference in all of our lives.

Ricky Esterquest
Disability consultant
towardsbetter.com.au

Inspiring and poetic, as well as down to earth and practical, this book by Joanne Lynam provides a generous insight into the role she has played in helping her daughter achieve her potential. Not seeking to take over Emma's life, Joanne worked *with* Emma to achieve what she wants. As she says, "the majesty to create and become whoever they want to be lies within ALL young people, if they are given the opportunity to realise it".

Margaret Rodgers
CEO, Community Resource Unit
cru.org.au

Joanne Lynam's book is a joy to read as she recounts her experiences in creating and raising her family. The story reveals how she grew to understand the importance of having positive expectations for her daughter Emma, who was born with Down syndrome, and how those expectations and actions built the good life that Emma now has. Jo has worked with Emma to make the transition from being a "client" of services to being a *citizen* in her community. This book will be an inspiration to parents of people with disabilities and to every other community member.

Ann Greer
Disability consultant, positive behaviour practitioner &
parent
Creative Action Factory

This story focuses on Emma – a person with a disability – and her mother Joanne, and it is captivating, inspiring and instructive. We follow them as they make their way through often-challenging periods in their lives in Australia and abroad. There is a lot to be learned from this book, and it will appeal to anyone interested in what it takes to be resourceful, creative and inspired while still living up to one's principles. Be prepared to be absorbed in an easily read, life-affirming memoir that enlightens us all about what makes "a good life".

Michael J Kendrick, PhD
International consultant in human services, speaker &
author
kendrickconsulting.org

Unputdownable! A raw but uplifting account of a mother's fight for basic rights for her family, Jo Lynam's *An Angel at My Door* is much more than a parent's journey – it's a call to action. Jo tackles difficult and confronting topics and shares how love turned to defiance, and resulted in great outcomes. Jo highlights the work we need to do as a society to ensure everyone is included and given the opportunity to shine. This book will touch many people and is essential reading for anyone wanting to work with people with disability. There are plenty of air-punch moments to get you going and to remind you of why you work in this sector.

Suzy Berry
Disability and mental health sector consultant
linkedin.com/in/suzy-berry-health-ndis-leadership

As an aunt to a beautiful niece living with Down syndrome, I've learnt so much from Joanne's sharing of her story. From learning to parent Emma well, to being her advocate, to ultimately getting out of the way to allow Emma to experience all the joys of adulthood (including international holidays, and business and home ownership)… hope is found. Our lives are enriched through the greater integration of society, and this is achieved by the hard-fought battles of people like Joanne who've gone before us.

Susie Holt
Radio presenter & speaker
lukeandsusie.com

Frustration and anger at prejudice and at an outdated system, as well as unwavering love and triumph, are the emotions Joanne Lynam takes you through in *An Angel at My Door*. Her determination to ensure that the world will *see* Emma is as heartbreaking as it is uplifting. Joanne is a terrific storyteller, enabling the reader to feel every emotion endured by a mother who wants the best for her children. A real page-turner and a life-altering book.

Natasha Buttler
Marketing strategist
boostmarketingservices.com.au

Having had the privilege of working with Emma and Jo over the years, I have personally been inspired by their resilience and by Emma's journey to success, happiness and independence. *An Angel at My Door* is thought-provoking, has powerful messages and includes wonderful resources for anyone who needs the confidence and support to trust that they can overcome hard times and enjoy a beautiful, purposeful life. An absolute must-read!

Rebecca Campbell
Head of Human Resources
queenslandcountry.bank

An Angel

AT MY DOOR

A mother's fight for her daughter
to live to her potential

JOANNE LYNAM

SWEETSPIRE **LITERATURE**
—— M A N A G E M E N T ——

Contents

Dedication

This book is dedicated to my three great teachers:

Roshan
Laksiri
&
Emma

Foreword

What risks are worth taking to create change in our world? What price is needed to produce the results that are worth fighting for? Would we be willing to make the kinds of sacrifices that were necessary if we wanted something good and decent for those we loved? Could we endure hardship and disappointment at every turn and yet press ahead, certain of eventual victory? Is it naïvely optimistic to expect change in one's own lifetime?

Joanne Lynam could not have foretold all that her life would bring. Yet through her intimate and very personal story we get to reflect on our own performance as we face the challenges and suffering that can often come our way. We get to ask ourselves whether or not we have the same guts and determination Joanne displays in overcoming every obstacle.

Joanne's story is largely about her fight for her children, one of whom is a daughter who has Down syndrome. To Joanne, the disability was irrelevant in the face of her immediate and all-consuming love for her baby, Emma. But what new hardships would they have to confront from a society that didn't share her daughter's worth?

We know people with disabilities face many negative ideas that prevent them from being seen as fully human. Whether perceived as perpetually immature and dependent (the "eternal child"), or as a source of pity, deserving of charity, or perhaps not deserving of a life at all, our ideas see only a magnified impairment, and this blocks out all other possibilities.

How is it that a child such as Emma, with numerous difficulties, could be unconditionally loved? And what kind of life would such a love produce for a child so embraced? Such contradictions make Joanne's story so compelling; none of her approaches to the challenges of raising a child with disabilities is according to the usual "script". But how could that be? Aren't the difficulties of a child born with significant disabilities overwhelming and insurmountable?

In reading this true story of a mother's fight for her daughter to live a typical life (that is, a life typically experienced by other people of her age who do not have disability), we end up confronting ideas that have limited the lives of a whole population of people, people we thought belonged elsewhere and not *with* us because they were not *like* us – not like "normal people". However, perhaps Joanne is in some way more exceptional than most, or her daughter more capable than most would think? We ask, "Surely such progress couldn't be achieved if I had a child like Emma?" Joanne's story assures us that if we view the world through the lens of possibility, and challenge limiting beliefs, we, too, can achieve success for and with people who have disability.

An Angel at My Door is a deeply personal, sometimes harrowing but often funny and inspiring story of a family's journey for a better life – a good life for their children against all the low and damning expectations of doctors, therapists, services and sometimes our communities.

As you will discover through the reading of Joanne's story, members of the public often stare when they see Emma venture into community settings without assistance. These are activities that are ordinary but, so far, largely unexperienced by someone with a disability, and by us who see it happen for the first time. Clearly, it will take several generations of such outliers to permanently alter the low expectations that are characteristically held about people with disabilities. Even some support organisations will have to reassess their positions, given that for generations they have used a person's impairment as a source of pity and entitlement for those families thusly affected, rather than using it to place that person at best advantage.

Later in her story, Joanne discovers the concept of Social Role Valorisation (SRV), a concept consistent with her long-held values and with her personal and professional efforts in the lives of other disadvantaged people. The principles of SRV reassure her that what she is seeking is truly good for Emma. When Emma is being visible and living to her potential, her gifts can contribute to others and reveal what is possible.

Opening up doors to the good things of life – and thereby normalising value and opportunity for people with disabilities – is a delicately iterated approach that requires many mid-course corrections; corrections that cannot always be anticipated. The process is tiring because it demands a watchful attention to detail. Such perseverance is necessary for success.

Joanne and Emma together walk this path of life. Their shared vision for Emma's life to be lived to its full embraces the clear potential that others, too, can learn and appreciate this and extract lessons crucial to a sustainable success.

Through this book and the joannelynam.com website, we are privileged to enter Joanne's and Emma's world and to appreciate the journey as well as the destination.

John Armstrong
SRV trainer & consultant
January 2021

PLANNING FOR
success

When you're the parent or carer of a person with a disability, you need to be supported.

That support can come from other people, but it also needs to come *from within you*. When you build a wellspring of resilience and strength you're able to be a powerful advocate for the person in your life.

To help fill your well, I've created a beautiful manifesto that you can print out. Read it every day and allow its words to support you.

HEAD HERE TO DOWNLOAD YOUR GIFT:

joannelynam.com/book-gift

ps As a **bonus**, I've also included a page of **inspiring affirmations** with your download.

A Note from Joanne

This is a story of hope, resilience and courage.

At its core, this is a book about social justice. While its lens is focused on disability, the same injustices apply to indigenous people, migrants, people with mental illness and the elderly – the invisible of society.

This book shares my journey of becoming a mother, and shares how the challenges I faced along that journey were the making of me and allowed for the unfolding of my true purpose. The story also reveals the abuse I experienced in my earlier life and the long shadow it cast over me.

This is a two-part book. While the first part isn't focused on disability, I encourage you to read it. You may have bought this book purely for its insights into disability – this is fine, and you may wish to skip to part two right now to discover those insights. However, in part one I share deeply personal and powerful stories from an earlier time in my life, and the lessons they provided are woven throughout the rest of the book and helped form my unusual and bold approach to parenting a child with a disability. I have chosen to include these very painful early experiences so that you might look at your own wounds in a new light, and to show how the quiet presence of resilience gently guided me through some very challenging times.

The second part of this book offers a different way of "looking" at disability. If you are a parent or a provider and you don't wish to simply follow the herd and stay safe – you instead dare to hold big dreams for the child in your care, no matter what anyone else tells you – then I am sure you will find my story helpful. Part two of the book is also a call to find the power of your resilience, just as I did when faced with the daily discrimination and rejection of my third child, Emma, who was born with a disability. I also share the thinking and planning I undertook that led to Emma being able to live to her potential. I reveal how, by not being willing to accept a second-class life for Emma, I was shown a way to help her craft a small business of her own.

What does it mean to live a good life? It's being engaged in meaningful work, being a valued member of society, having a safe home to live in, and having loving friends and family. These are the things that we all take for granted as we go about our everyday lives. But when a person with an intellectual disability achieves the "ordinary" things of life, it is extraordinary.

Where many people couldn't see the person, and instead saw only the disability, I saw gifts and a way forward to a good life.

I feel it is important to address a concern that some people, particularly those within the SRV community (which you'll learn about later) may have with the title of this book. The "angel" of An Angel at My Door is not Emma. Rather, it is the gentle presence that we could call consciousness, the universe or God. When you come to read part two of this book, you'll discover how this presence revealed itself and foretold what was to lie ahead.

It is my sincere hope that this book shines a light for you, a light that helps you along your journey to finding a good life for the precious person in your world who has a disability.

With love and gratitude

Joanne

PS I would love to stay in touch with you – please head to joannelynam.com to find the link to my Facebook page, and to discover all of the resources that I've compiled for you.

PPS You will also find a handy resources section at the end of this book.

Part 1

A Contract Written Long Ago...

CHAPTER 1

It Happened to Me, Too*

*"Don't be pushed around by the fears in your mind.
Be led by the dreams in your heart."*

— *Roy T Bennett*

This book is about the journey that we, as a family, agreed to take with our daughter and sister, Emma. A journey that, I believe, was agreed upon long before we came to this earth.

With the benefit of hindsight, it's clear to me that this journey was strengthened by my resilience. Resilience provided me with the courage and strength to continue when it all seemed too difficult.

I was born and bred in a small mining town called Mt Isa in north-west Queensland, Australia. I am the eldest of four children. My childhood couldn't be described as happy; rather, it was one where my physical needs were met in an environment devoid of any expression of love, or of any encouragement for wanting to aspire to something different.

From the first time I saw a drummer as a little girl I knew I wanted to play drums. However, when I expressed this, my parents told me, "Don't be silly. Girls don't play drums". When I was a teenager, my parents bought me a guitar – I think they felt this might give me a new focus and change my mind. It didn't.

In my happy place, age 17

While on a family holiday in Brisbane (about 20 hours' drive from my hometown), one of my cousins introduced me to his drum teacher. The music teacher, Fred (not his real name), could see that I was very keen. He showed me a couple of simple first steps and suggested that I practise on an old drum kit in the back room of his music school. For the next four weeks I spent every day in that back room, practising everything that Fred showed me.

As the end of the four weeks drew near, Fred asked me how serious I was about playing drums. He said it might be possible for me to get a 12-month scholarship that would allow me to stay in Brisbane and continue with my studies. My parents were not happy about leaving me in the city on my own, but they did eventually agree, on the condition that I live with my grandma. I loved my grandma very much so this wasn't an issue for me.

I absolutely loved playing the drums and spent a lot of time each day practising patterns and rhythms over and over until I had perfected them. My favourite time of day was when I put the stereo on full blast and drummed along to music. I responded intuitively to the sounds, and playing the drums often felt like an out-of-body experience.

Although my studies were going well, my relationship with my parents wasn't. When the 12-month scholarship was up they insisted that I come back home. However, I had no intention of leaving my studies at that point. Mum and Dad said that if this was the path I chose then they would not provide any financial assistance. My dad said, "Nice girls don't play drums. Come home, Jo". I was determined to stay. So, to support myself, I began playing in bands of an evening.

In theory, this sounded like a good idea. However, in the 1970s the music industry was very male dominated and an 18-year-old female drummer was not welcome. In the beginning I was often rejected by bands purely because of my gender. But I was a quick learner and I figured out a way to get work. I would take my gear to a venue and set up before a band arrived. Then, I would head off, and come back closer to the gig time so that I could hang around inside the venue but not approach the band. Once they started panicking about the whereabouts of their drummer, I would stroll up and introduce myself as the drummer (no longer as Joanne, but as Jo). I would then hear their predictable excuses about how people wouldn't be able to hear me. To this I would say, "Tell you what. How about I play the first bracket, and if you're not happy I will get you a new drummer?" I was never sent home after that.

My teacher had the idea of making a record of my drumming because he thought this could help kick off my career. Musician friends of his accompanied me on the recording and I performed a drum solo on the A side.

I also appeared on a number of TV shows (including *A Crooke Affair*) to promote the record, and a couple of newspapers (including *The Australian*) covered the story.

Life had a now familiar rhythm of theory, practice and preparation for exams. But playing drums made me feel truly alive; it was almost like an addiction. I just had to play. If I went a day without playing I would be itching to get to my kit.

However, there was a darker side to life as a female musician. Many people, particularly men, thought that as a woman I had no business playing drums in a band. Some changed their minds after listening to me play. Some were just rude and made sexual advances and were offended that I didn't take them up on their offer.

One Saturday, just days after a newspaper story (in which I was called "The Little Drummer Girl") was published, I was offered a wedding gig. It was at a football club, for a band I hadn't played with before. As I'd come to expect, the band members were less than thrilled to have a young girl playing with them. I tossed them the usual deal – give me the first bracket and if you aren't happy, I will go. They were happy and didn't send me home.

As a group, they weren't a bad lot. They were just a bit challenged by my presence in a role they believed was meant purely for males. Sometimes the casual bands I played with would invite me to sit with them at their table, but not this band. So in the breaks I sat at the end of the bar. During the first break three guys came over to me and said, "Hey, aren't you that little drummer girl who was in the paper the other day?" I said, "Yes, I am". At first, they were polite and said I played well... for a girl. But as the night wore on, they became more insistent on buying me drinks, despite my telling them I didn't drink.

As the night came to a close, at about 1am, I felt very uneasy about these three men. I asked the guys in the band whether they would mind hanging around until I had packed up. One of them said, "What? Are you scared of the dark? That's why girls can't play drums. Packing up is all part of it, doll". So I packed up my kit and attempted to get it all into my car. This was no simple feat, as I had an eight-piece drum kit with four cymbals and stands. I hadn't been allowed to bring it in through the front so I had to take it out the back into the carpark.

I had almost finished packing when the three guys from earlier that night appeared beside my car. I felt an absolute terror run through my body. I was raped, sodomised and badly beaten by all three of them, and left unconscious in the carpark. I woke up on the ground with my clothes torn and scattered around the carpark. To this day I still recall trying to find my clothes and put them back on, even though they were torn. Perhaps it was shock... I don't know. Somehow I drove back to Grandma's house, and I spent literally hours in the shower washing and washing myself, as if I might be able to somehow wash the stain of those three men off me. The next morning I went to the hospital because I had been torn and I was still bleeding. In the years after the rape I could not count the number of times I wished I could go back in time and just leave my drum kit inside the hotel. I could have gone back the next day to collect it.

At first the doctor who attended to me was very nice because he knew this wasn't an accident (which is what I had said had happened to me). However, when I told him I was a drummer in a band, his attitude changed completely. He made the comment, "Well, what did you think would happen? When you behave like one of the boys... you prob- ably got what you deserved". I remember feeling confused by that comment – I was raped but I was in the wrong? One of the hardest things to overcome was hearing my father's words play over and over in my head: "You're a good girl, Jo. Good girls don't play drums". I felt broken and beaten and I didn't understand what I had done to deserve this. My head was filled constantly by the scene, with it playing over and over in my mind. I kept thinking, "I should have listened to Dad; he was right. I am not a good girl. This is all my fault and if I can't fix it, no one can".

Due to the nature of the injuries sustained in the attack, I stayed away from the drumming school for about eight weeks. I didn't want anyone to know or even suspect what had happened to me and I didn't want to talk about it. In fact, I went to a church, lit a candle and made a vow that I would never speak of what had happened to me.

It would be another 26 years before I did speak of it, and another seven years before I was able to let it go.

After the rape I still enjoyed playing drums, just not in bars and hotels. In fact, I found it increasingly difficult to maintain my life in the city. I knocked back more work than I could afford because I was simply terrified, every moment of the day. I kept thinking that the three men might be in the club or bar I was working in. I saw their faces everywhere I went.

Money had become a very big challenge and I almost lost my drum kit to the HP (hire purchase) company because I couldn't make the repayments. At this point I felt completely broken. I decided to go home to my parents.

When I saw the stories of sexual abuse of women that led to the "Me Too" movement, I wept and wept. It felt as though I was weeping not only for myself, but for all the women over thousands of years who had been forced to silently carry the burden and trauma of their abuse. They also carried the

burden of society's silence and of its not wanting to acknowledge the harm that has been inflicted on so many women.
A burden that implied they were somehow responsible for
what had happened to them. The burden of the weight of
comments like those of the doctor I saw the morning after
the rape, a doctor who made himself the judge and jury and
found me guilty. Guilty of stepping outside of my allotted
place as a young woman. The "Me Too" movement fills me
with hope – hope that we have finally reached the day when
women are valued and treated equally in society, including
within the justice system.

Twenty-six years ago I spoke to a counsellor about what
had happened to me, and she asked if I had ever thought
about going to the police at the time. Aside from the fact
that the three men responsible knew where I studied and
had threatened to get me if I did go to the police, my experience with the doctor showed me that I would not have
found any support if I had wanted to seek justice. Out of
fear, I had made the decision to remain silent – like so many
women before me.

CHAPTER 2

A Precious Gift

"The past has no power until we visit it."

— Joanne Lynam

After I had been back home in Mt Isa for a while, I got a job with a mining company. It was there that I met Greg. He was tall and handsome and had a quiet gentle way about him. After our first date I invited him to a family gathering. Nothing like throwing a newcomer right into the total chaos of my family's gatherings! My two brothers teased Greg relentlessly about always agreeing with Mum, and they called him "Silence" because he didn't say much when he was amid the noise and arguments of my family. When I met Greg's family for the first time I could understand why he found my family so "full on". Greg is one of six children and, seriously, all six of them (including their partners and children) could be gathered and you wouldn't have known they were there – they were so quiet. Greg and I married in April 1980, despite coming from very different families.

Young and in love, at our engagement

I had wanted to start a family right away. I don't really know why, but I felt a strong, urgent pull to become a mum. However, my journey to motherhood was not destined to be straightforward. We were told that it was very unlikely I would become pregnant, as we both had fertility issues. Greg and I talked a lot about this and what was important to us. It wasn't important that any child was biologically ours, and he/she didn't have to look like us. We saw that there were plenty of children in the world already, so why not take care of and love a child that didn't have a home and family? We decided to adopt a child from Sri Lanka. At the time I couldn't have explained, in any logical way, why I felt drawn to Sri Lanka.

Now I understand that I was being pulled to Sri Lanka by a commitment I had made long before I came to this earth. I made an agreement with my two sons that I would be their mother. No matter where they were, I would find them and keep my commitment.

Our first adoption had all the usual bureaucratic paperwork and delays that one expects when dealing with government departments. But apart from that, the process went relatively well.

Just after lunch one day in November 1984, I received a phone call telling us about our son, who was just seven weeks old. His name was Asitha Roshan. We ultimately chose to use Roshan as his first name. Our next phone bill was pretty big because I think we called everyone we knew to share our news.

I will never forget the first time I saw Roshan. I felt my heart beating so fast. It was a wild mix of excitement and a sudden fearful thought of, "What if he doesn't like me?" As I took him in my arms, he smelled so wonderful. I sat down and laid him on my legs and unwrapped this tiny little 4lb bundle.

He had been asleep and as I unwrapped him his big dark eyes opened and looked at me with such a serious

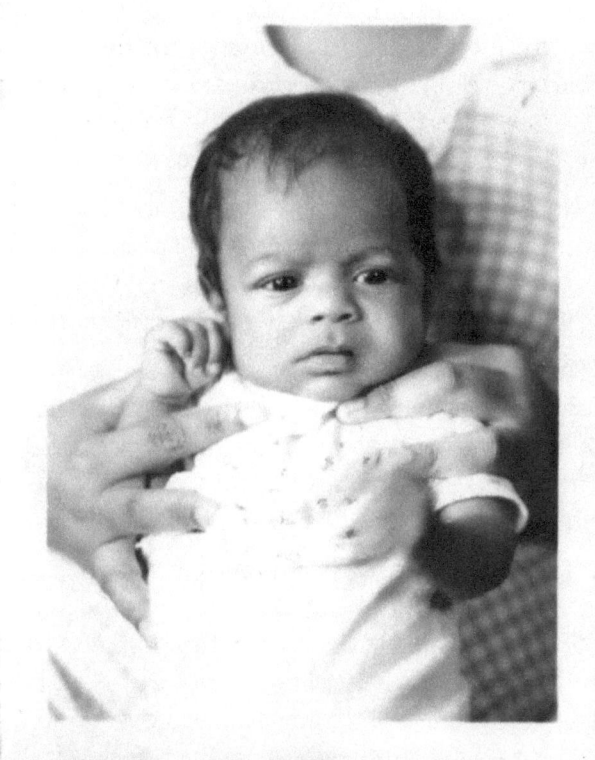

Roshan at eight weeks of age

little-man look. He had beautiful wavy hair down past his ears. He was so, so beautiful and I was in awe of the immediate love I felt for him.

In Sri Lanka, the adoption process required the relinquishing mother and the adopting parents to go for an interview with what was then called the Department of Child Care and Probation. Then, if the department was satisfied that everything was in order, the relinquishing mother and adopting parents had to appear in court before a judge, with all of the correct paperwork. The Queensland government had an agreement with the Sri Lankan government that recognised the ruling of Sri Lankan courts, and this meant that Roshan was legally ours when the court hearing was complete.

But before the formalities of the hearing and the adoption were complete, we had a chance to experience the beauty of that tiny island and its warm people. We left the heat of Colombo and enjoyed a few relaxing days in the hillside cool of Kandy. This area is where tea is grown in Sri Lanka.

One Sunday we took the suggestion of the family with whom we were staying and went a little way south of Colombo to Mt Lavinia. It was there that we visited a beautiful old hotel perched high on the rocks and overlooking the sea. I will never forget the smorgasbord lunch that day. I have never seen so much food in one place, and all of it was wonderful. Sri Lanka was a wonderful, exciting mix of cultures and chaos, and whenever I hear anyone speak about it I am immediately transported back to the tiny teardrop-shaped island.

On the day of the court hearing there were lengthy delays, so we went back to the home of our hosts to sit in the cool. We took Roshan and his mother with us. She very kindly let me take her photo so that when Roshan was older I could show him the woman who made our dreams come true through her sacrifice.

When the court hearing was finished I handed Roshan back to his mother so that she might have the opportunity to say goodbye to her son. She quietly took him and started whispering to him, so Greg and I moved away to give her privacy. She then walked very determinedly towards us and thrust Roshan into my arms before disappearing into the crowd. While Greg and I could do nothing to change the system in Sri Lanka, it was absolutely gut-wrenching to watch her just disappear into the crowd, wondering how she would cope and if she had support.

I have often wondered if Roshan's mother thinks about him as much as I think about her. If we had been given a choice, it would have been nice to have had some ongoing contact with her. This would have kept the door open for Roshan, should he ever choose to look for his family. If he does ever make this decision it is with my absolute blessing and support.

When we returned to Sri Lanka for our second adoption we stayed with the same family. They told me that Roshan's biological grandmother had one day shown up at the gate and asked about her grandson, Asitha Roshan. The family said they gave her some of the many photos I had sent them. They told me she was very happy to see Roshan looking so well and clearly loved, and she could tell he had not been sold into slavery as she had first thought.

Every decision we make in life has a consequence. We are responsible for whatever happens as a result of having made that decision. Stepping back onto Australian soil, I felt very aware of the responsibility I had in bringing my beautiful brown boy into a country that might not always welcome him. Also, our decision to adopt changed each of our families and how they saw themselves – overnight they became mixed-race families.

It was a long and challenging flight home, with Roshan crying most of the way. In hindsight, I probably should have

Arriving home with our precious baby boy, Roshan

just told the airline, "I won't be needing an actual seat as I will be walking most of the way", which is pretty much what I did because Roshan was very unsettled for most of the flight.

Now we were finally a little family, and I was overwhelmed with feelings of sheer joy and love...

CHAPTER 3

From Heartache to Heaven

"The bond that links your true family is not one of blood,
but of respect and joy in each other's life."

— Richard Bach

Motherhood and I were meant to be. I loved everything about being Roshan's mum. When Roshan was a baby, one of my favourite times was sitting with him for hours in the rocking chair, just rocking. It didn't matter to me that he wasn't asleep and it didn't seem to matter to him; we both just rocked together in the chair. One day I had an insight that, in fact, the creaking and rocking motion of the chair was a little like the action of a loom weaving in and out. As we rocked together, we were gently weaving the different strands of our lives together.

By the time Roshan was two years of age, we had submitted an application to the Queensland child services department to adopt another child from Sri Lanka. A few months later we relocated to a very small mining community of just 1500 people.

After we had unpacked and settled into our new home, we made contact with the department regarding the processing of our paperwork. This second adoption was fraught with bureaucratic ineptitude and heartbreak, with one department refusing to help us and another losing paperwork. In the end, the way forward was only achieved through the intervention of the minister at the time, who issued a ministerial. (This is a directive that orders the workers to leave all other matters and complete this matter, in the time frame stated by the minister.)

Our paperwork had finally made its way to Sri Lanka. But our challenges were far from over. A baby-buying racket had been uncovered just outside of Colombo. While it was a good thing that this awful practice had been found and stopped, it had a huge ripple effect throughout the entire country. We were caught up in it. We could not get our paperwork back and we didn't know if we could go forward.

Because of the support and kindness of members of the Sri Lankan community here in Australia, I was eventually able to meet with a Sri Lankan minister who was enjoying a holiday in Australia. The minister was a warm and understanding person who agreed to try to help us once she was back in Sri Lanka.

After this, several children were allocated to us. Unfortunately, each of these children had medical issues and the Queensland government would not grant approval for them to come to Australia.

This time was like being on an emotional roller-coaster, with euphoric moments of hope followed by the grief and despair of yet another setback. There were many times during this period when I felt utterly defeated, and overwhelmed by the sheer size of the challenges we were facing.

... I felt utterly defeated, and overwhelmed by the sheer size of the challenges we were facing.

As a couple, Greg and I were at breaking point. We argued constantly – about everything. The fire that was burning our relationship was the immense weight of the challenges of trying to get our second child. I spent hours on the phone going back and forth with Australian departments and then phoning Sri Lanka to try to get answers. If I wasn't dealing with departments on the phone I was driving into town to speak with them. One particular night still burns bright in my memory. Greg was tired after a long day at work, and he came home to find me upset and crying about not being able to make progress. Greg is usually a very patient man but this night he lost it and was yelling at me, "Just forget about it, Jo. It's not going to happen". I was confused and frustrated and lashed out, saying, "Well, at least I am not giving up".

But in my calmer moments, usually early in the morning, something much greater than me or my personality would visit me and help me see myself with two beautiful children from Sri Lanka. I have no idea where this quiet knowing came from but its presence helped me to hang on.

Finally, after what felt like a lifetime of struggle and heartbreak, we were offered a little boy called Laksiri. His exact age was unknown because he did not have a birth certificate, but we were told he was probably around two years of age. Laksiri had begun his life in an overcrowded government orphanage where he, like so many of the children, suffered severe malnutrition. He lapsed into a coma and was taken to a nutrition centre about two hours from Colombo. It was from this nutrition centre that we adopted Laksiri. The centre received some financial support from Australia and there were some Australian nurses volunteering there.

The first time I saw Laksiri, my heart ached for him. He was sitting on the floor with a small group of children of about the same age. As he looked up at me with his beautiful brown eyes that were filled with tears and fear, I struggled to hold back my own tears. I just wanted to scoop him up into my arms and tell him that it was all going to be fine. But I could see that he was very wary and fearful of us. So I took the advice of the Aussie nurses and took a slowly, slowly approach.

Each morning we would make the two-hour trip to the nutrition centre to see Laksiri and try to get to know him a little better. After lunch the children would take a rest. At this time I would usually go down to the nursery and help the Aussie nurses with the babies. This part of the orphanage was always busy and they were often under-staffed. Being with the nurses was always very helpful because they would share little bits of information about Laksiri. I would also feed babies or just play with them.

One afternoon shortly before our court date I went down to the baby section to chat and to see if help was needed. To my horror there was a little boy of about 12 months of age who had arrived overnight. He was so malnourished that he looked like a skeleton wrapped in skin. His eyes were like lifeless hollows in his sunken face. I was moved to tears at the very sight of this poor little boy. He wasn't the only baby who had arrived overnight, so I asked what I could do to help. One of the nurses told me that there was nothing to be done for this poor little soul. They had been trying to get nourishment into him but he couldn't keep it down. "He is dying", she said. I will never understand where I got the courage to go over and pick him up and hold him – but I did. The nurse said, "Jo, there is nothing you can do for him now. Don't do this to yourself, it will torture you". But I knew I would be tortured if I just walked away, so I stayed.

There was one thing I could do for this little boy. I could hold him and show him love as he slipped away. If only for a short time, he had arms to hold him and a soft voice to carry him to the other side. The nurse was right. The memory of this little boy, whose name I didn't even know, has tortured me.

Laksiri at two years of age, enjoying a feed at the nutrition centre

During my time in Sri Lanka I learned many things about the value of human life. In the orphanage, I realised the incredible resilience of the human spirit. I had taken lots of toys and books with us to keep Roshan entertained in Sri Lanka. One day I had set up Roshan out on the veranda with his bubble pipe. While I was making lunch I heard him laughing and calling out to someone. I looked out to see him blowing bubbles down to the little boy who lived across the way. They were both having so much fun without either of them understanding the other.

At another time, on a train, we sat beside a mum and her little girl and within minutes Roshan and the little girl were engaged in play. Again, no words were needed – just two little children seeing a friend with whom to spend a passing moment. The resilience of children carries them far above the battleground of life. I remember thinking that perhaps the world might see a lot less war and strife if children were in charge.

Arrangements were made for one of the "akkas" (which means "sisters" and was the term used for local girls who worked in the orphanage) to bring Laksiri to Colombo for the court hearing. When she arrived with Laksiri, he was asleep. Akka explained that he had cried most of the way until he fell asleep.

The court hearing was swift – thankfully. We took Akka, Roshan and Laksiri to lunch and then made our way home.

Akka needed to make her way back to the orphanage so that she wouldn't be out after curfew. When Laksiri realised Akka was leaving, his little face crumbled and he cried and reached out for her. Tears fell down her gentle face as she blessed Laksiri and wished us all well. I will be forever haunted by the memory of this day. We were all in tears while Laksiri kept calling out for Akka. Standing out in the courtyard as the afternoon slipped away, I felt the judging eyes of the neighbours boring into my body. The courtyard seemed to be closing in on me and my little family. Laksiri's cries burned into me like hot metal. I knew I would need all of my resilience and courage to help him adjust to his new home.

Back then, in 1987, the Sri Lankan government did not recognise children without a birth certificate as citizens. Laksiri travelled to Australia as a stateless person on a one-way travel document. Such an indignity for a little boy. But he has grown into a kind and generous person and a fine Australian citizen and a son I love with all of my heart, a son of whom I am very proud.

Greg and I have always tried to give our sons a good life, a life of opportunity and with choice about the direction they could take. I could not give them LIFE; their biological mothers gave them that gift. I am forever indebted to the women who, with courage and grace, gave me my two beautiful sons.

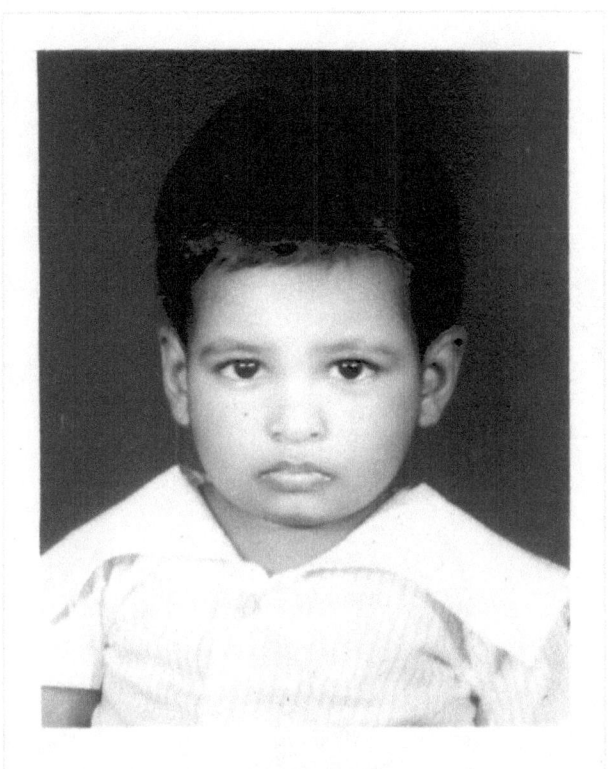

Laksiri, ready to fly to Australia

My Brown-Skin Boy

My beautiful brown-skin boy,
given to me by another's hand,
of sorrow and love from a far-off land.
Over the seas of time did our lives cross,
were you taken now, I would die of loss.
To watch you sleeping so peaceful and still,
there is no more room in my heart to fill.
To your brown-skin mother, I remain in your debt,
though the years may pass I will never forget.
Remember, my brown-skin boy,
you did not grow under my heart,
but in it.

Joanne Lynam, 1987

CHAPTER 4

The Gift of Difference

*"Acceptance is what we wish for ourselves
and often deny others."*

— Susan L Taylor

L iving in a small community meant that everyone knew who we were and that we had been trying to adopt our second child from Sri Lanka. However, for quite some time Laksiri was frightened of strangers who came to the house. The first few months were challenging for all of us as we struggled to understand and comfort Laksiri. Adjusting to a new home must have been very difficult for him because not one thing was familiar to him.

One of the greatest challenges at this time was language – Laksiri only spoke Sinhala and although I knew a small amount of conversational Sinhala it was not enough to help him.

I knew I had to get on top of the language issues because it was very clearly causing all of us problems. When we didn't understand him he would get very upset and throw himself on the floor. I could not count the number of nights on which I fell into bed completely exhausted after a day of this kind of behaviour. I would often lie in bed with tears streaming down my face, asking, "How can I help him?" It was just heartbreaking.

Then one morning I had an idea. I got the camera and went around taking photos of everything in the house. This was a game-changer. When Laksiri was struggling to be understood I would say to him, "Where is your book? Show Mummy what you want". By spending time with him each day looking at his book and saying the names of the items, he started to grasp some English.

Laksiri was not a reading, painting kind of kid. He was my little action man. He always wanted to be on the trike, in the sandpit with trucks, or on the swing.

Within 12 months we had got on top of his health issues, including anaemia. Now that he was well, he began to show us his strong, feisty personality. It was this strength and feistiness that gave him the will to hang on when his life was hanging in the balance back at the nutrition centre.

Once Laksiri began to speak a little English, he found it much easier to settle in. Going to kindergarten was one of the best things for him. It was so helpful with his language development and with making friends, and all of this made him feel more comfortable in his new life.

There are many wonderful things about living in such a small town, including the freedom children have to play and safely walk down the street with friends, and knowing everyone. However, life here wasn't all sweetness. You know what they say about small towns: "There's not much to do in a small town but, gee, there's always lots to talk about". Roshan, Laksiri and a beautiful Cambodian family were the only people of colour in town.

There were some people who were concerned about our sons being in the community. I remember a teacher telling me that a parent had expressed concern about Roshan being in her child's class because Roshan had come from a country at war. This mother wanted her child to be safe. After speaking with the teacher, I went home and cried but I knew I would need to address this issue. Initially, families were very wary of us and our adopted sons. After the initial hurt had settled, I had an insight. Though this mother didn't know it, we actually had a great deal in common – the desire to keep our children safe, the hopes that they would have a bright future, and our deep love for them.

When we first arrived, families were very reluctant to allow their children to come to our home to play with Roshan. Lots of invitations were given out before anyone came to play. At that time I just didn't know how to reassure people that my son wasn't a threat, and that children all like to play. Once, the manager of the local pool quietly told me that someone had complained about my boys being in the pool. The concern? "They could spread infection." As a mum, I was devastated by these kinds of comments. But something in me told me that they were just fearful, and that I could help them see things differently. I had no idea where this understanding came from – certainly not from the personality called "me". This had come from somewhere way beyond me.

The way forward came one night when the boys were both asleep. The house was quiet and still. In fact, the whole town felt still and peaceful. There was just the almost-hypnotic sound of crickets. I put down my book and moved out into the carport, where I sat looking out into the darkness. One of the great advantages of living away from cities is the incredible beauty of the night sky. On this particular night, the sky was like rich black velvet. The stars seemed so bright and close, as if I could just about reach out and touch them. I became very still, and a way forward came quietly to me... almost as though it had come from the blackness of the night.

I saw that the way to get people in the community to accept and embrace my boys was to get *involved* and to show people how we are so much more alike than different. After this I took every opportunity to speak about how much we have in common and how this common humanity can help us all. Greg and I made sure we joined every committee that was working towards improving the preschool, kindy or school.

At one point, I was on the preschool committee and suggested that we host an international food fair. It was a great, fun way to raise money for the preschool but, of equal importance, it also would bring the community together. With a little prompting about family cultural heritage, so many people came forward with stories of their cultural background and offered to help. We began to plan for the night and cook up a storm. In the end, the fair was a hit! We raised more money than we imagined and the preschool was able to purchase a much-needed pergola. However, more importantly (at least to me), people were coming together for the good of their community.

While we are not at all a religious family, I also did some cooking for the little local church because I reasoned it was another opportunity to build bridges of connection. On one occasion I baked a traditional Sri Lankan Christmas cake. This cake is something quite special and weighs 7lbs when it is finished. It was offered as a raffle prize and the winner was a very quiet lady I hadn't met before. A year later I was back with another cake to raffle and the lady who won it the year before returned to buy more tickets – she hoped to win it again. She was certainly good for ticket sales.

I knew that bringing people together to share food and stories would form the roadmap to a strong, united

Our cheeky boys, Laksiri (age four) & Roshan (age six)

community. It's pretty hard to hate someone while you share food and stories with them.

During the six years we spent in this little community we hosted many curry nights at our home and had many wonderful evenings with beautiful people. I liked to think that while we were feeding their bodies curry, their minds were being fed a vision of the strength of togetherness.

Part 2

Stepping into a New Reality

CHAPTER 5

Tears of Joy

"You don't choose your family.
They are God's gift to you, as you are to them."

— Desmond Tutu

In 1991 Greg took up a position in Papua New Guinea. My parents had moved to Townsville after retiring, so we relocated there – I had hoped that by being in Townsville my parents might come to know and love my sons.

Townsville gave me more outlets to explore my growing spiritual yearnings. I became a regular at a local meditation centre. At the end of 1993, members of the meditation centre planned to travel to India to spend time in an ashram. I decided to join them.

Throughout my life I have had dreams that have foretold something that later happened. Just two weeks before my trip to the ashram, I had an amazing dream that was clearly guiding me in some way, or warning me.

In the dream I was travelling in a car with some other dev-otees. I was sitting in the back seat. Suddenly I had a clear knowing that the road was about to make a really sharp turn, back in the reverse direction. I felt very alarmed and was concerned that the driver might not know about this turn. I worried whether or not the car could negotiate it safely. However, the car smoothly made the sharp turn. I watched the road ahead through the front windscreen, and the road suddenly disappeared. I felt my stomach drop as the car went down a very steep hill. We continued along the road, experiencing even more steep rises and falls.

When I woke, I had a strange feeling about this dream. The feeling stayed with me all day, and the next. What did it mean? Before I knew it I was packing for my trip to India and was on my way, the dream forgotten. As the plane touched down in Mumbai, the dream suddenly came back to me. I felt that it was predicting something. But I had no idea what that could be, and this made me feel uneasy.

My four weeks in the ashram was a heady mix of bliss and chaos. With 10,000 visitors, there were plenty of challenges. There was one particular day that I will always remember. It was the day the guru gave me a spiritual name – "Shree Devi", meaning "one of light". While I was very happy to have been given the name, it somehow felt like it carried with it a certain responsibility.

The ashram is known for its beautiful gardens, and I liked to walk through them each day, usually in the morning. One morning I came across one of the swamis (monks) talking to a group of people. He was telling them a story about a saint who was very kind and caring to his ageing parents. The saint knew that taking care of his elderly parents was his service to God. The saint had a difficult life and had prayed long and hard to God to relieve him of suffering. Then, one night, God came to the saint and told him it was his time to depart. But he told God, "First I must take care of my family".

The swami then went on to explain to this group that there is no greater path than to truly serve one's family. He then said that sometimes householders think that monks and swamis do greater work. But he said the life of a householder could take one to enlightenment just as easily as the life of a monk. This little story that I apparently "overheard" stayed with me throughout my stay in the ashram. Several times during my stay I pondered on what it meant. But a true understanding of it would not come to me for many years.

For most of my time in the ashram I felt a little unwell. I was constantly nauseous, and I put this down to the different food and water.

When I returned home I still had that same constant nausea. I decided to go to the doctor and get it checked out. My doctor listened as I told her where I had been and how I was feeling. Her first question was, "Could you be pregnant?" I said, "Well, after 14 years of marriage, that seems unlikely". But she did the test, and then said, "You are pregnant, Jo". I was stunned. A million questions ran through my head, the loudest being, "How, after all of these years?" I sat in my car and just cried. Tears of joy and gratitude flowed down my face. After all of these years of hoping it just might happen for me, as it had for so many of my family and friends, I couldn't believe it really had happened.

Greg was over the moon when I phoned him in Papua New Guinea to tell him. I realised I should probably wait a little while before telling anyone else, but I was so happy and just couldn't keep my amazing news to myself. Within a few hours everyone knew. Roshan was very excited about the idea of a brother or sister; Laksiri thought it might be OK but commented that he would really prefer a dog.

The following week I went for an ultrasound. I was nine weeks' pregnant. At that time the baby was in a transverse position but the doctor assured me that most babies move around.

"Could you be pregnant?" I said, "Well, after 14 years of marriage, that seems unlikely". But she did the test, and then said, "You are pregnant, Jo".

Three mornings after that I sat for my morning meditation and asked a question: "Is this a little girl?" I was curious, as I had a strong feeling I was carrying a girl. I placed my hands on my stomach. Suddenly I had a very clear vision of myself giving birth. There was someone with me but I didn't see who. I could only see their hands lifting up the baby in front of me. There was my little girl and it was very clear that she had Down syndrome.

In that moment it felt as though the entire universe held its breath. I felt so still and peaceful, in a way that I had never felt before – not even in the ashram at the feet of the guru had I felt this kind of stillness. There was a beautiful sense of being gently, lightly held. I also felt tremendous love – not for anyone in particular, but for everyone and everything. I had the sense that I was being guided by something. I knew everything would be alright. It felt as though I had been sitting for a long time, but in reality it had been quite a brief time. I sat for a while longer, taking in what had just happened. In that moment I realised that the dream I had before going to the ashram was, in fact, clearly showing me the direction my life was about to take. I had a strong inner knowing that this change would be about more than just another baby; it was going to be seismic shift in my life.

As I stood up to go and make breakfast for the boys, I knew with an absolute peaceful KNOWING that my baby girl had Down syndrome. I didn't feel frightened or upset, just peaceful and so grateful to have been given this insight. Greg was away at the time so I didn't mention it during our phone calls. But when he came home I told him what I had experienced in meditation, and that I knew the baby had Down syndrome. He said, "It's alright, we will be OK. But you are probably just worrying".

By the time I was 18 weeks' pregnant it was obvious something wasn't right. I was way too big for 18 weeks. A specialist checked an ultrasound, which he said revealed that the baby had a duodenal atresia. This means that the developing foetus is swallowing but nothing can get past its stomach because of atresia (a closure in the passage), so the fluid comes back up. I was advised that my baby would require surgery shortly after birth to repair this condition.

Duodenal atresia also causes a condition in the mother called polyhydramnios – this means there is too much fluid around the baby. Because of this it was very difficult to feel any movement, so I was going to the hospital every other day to have the baby's heart monitored. By 30 weeks I was the size of a woman at 40 weeks. My gynaecologist decided to remove some of the now four litres of amniotic fluid around the baby. She explained the risks associated with removing some of the fluid, but I went ahead because I was so uncomfortable. As she was draining off the fluid, she asked if she could send some for an amniocentesis. I had a strong sense that she thought the baby might have Down syndrome. But I gave my permission and said nothing about my knowing that my baby did indeed have Down syndrome.

At another appointment my doctor asked me if I knew what trisomy 21 was. We didn't have the results of the test yet but I felt that she was trying to "prepare me for the worst". I told her I knew trisomy 21 was Down syndrome. I also shared what I had seen in meditation about my baby having Down syndrome. She gently touched my arm and left the room.

I made it as far as 32 weeks. It was a Saturday, and Greg was due home later that day from Papua New Guinea. But he got held up by fog and didn't make it home until the Monday.

After lunch I had laid down for a little rest. When I stood up to check on the boys, my waters broke. When I say they broke, I mean it was like a fire hydrant. A friend took me to the hospital and called Mum and Dad to come to get the boys.

An ultrasound revealed that the baby was still in a transverse position, so I was prepared for a C-section. Because I had only just eaten, a general anaesthetic wasn't possible. So I had an epidural, which gave me the opportunity to be awake and see my baby.

I remember looking out of the window just as they got started and seeing that there was a sudden sprinkle of rain. I took this as a blessing on my baby girl. When Emma was born one of the nurses quickly held her up to show her to me. I looked at her and saw the face of the little baby in my meditation. Without intending to I said, "Oh, my beautiful little Down syndrome angel". I watched as a look went between the staff in the theatre; they obviously didn't expect me to know that my baby had Down syndrome.

My doctor sat with me in theatre and explained that she had received the results of the amniocentesis the day before, and they revealed that the baby did, in fact, have Down syndrome. In the recovery room a nurse asked me whether or not I was alright. Did I understand what the doctor had explained to me? When I said that I understood and that I knew I was having a baby with Down syndrome, she was a bit surprised. I then explained how I had known. She was a very lovely caring nurse and asked if I wanted to see the social worker because there would be a lot to take in. She said that I had a difficult road ahead of me.

I then heard myself say something, and I had no idea where it came from. I told her, "This little girl is not going to be hidden away; you are going to know about her". Over the years since Emma's birth I couldn't count how many times I have had conversations with other mothers about their experiences of having a baby with Down syndrome. I have witnessed the pain and shock that, without exception, each mother I've spoken to went through. They were grappling with the reality that their dream of a "normal" healthy baby was now a nightmare of dealing with the many challenges of having a child with a disability. Every time I have been honoured with the gift of a mum sharing her story, I have always felt so blessed that I was spared the shock and grief that so many families have experienced. I always knew that I was having a child with Down syndrome, and that there was no mistake. I was given a knowing that this child was the perfect child for me.

When I got back to my room that day, Dad and Mum were there. Emma was in intensive care by then. Dad asked how the baby was and if everything else was alright. I said, "Well, the baby has Down syndrome". Soft tears ran down Dad's face as he hugged me and said, "I am so sorry". I remember telling him, "Don't be sorry, Dad. Everything will be fine". I had no idea where this crystal-clear knowing came from.

Mum, being the wellspring of human kindness that she is, went off her head. She started screaming, "Look what you've done now. It wasn't bad enough you bringing shame to the family when you adopted two black children. Now, here you are again bringing shame to the family with a disabled child". She just kept screaming, "Why didn't you get the test?" In the end, the nurse in my room asked Mum several times to calm down, but Mum pushed her away. So the nurse called security to remove her from my room. Mum didn't come back to the hospital to see me or Emma. Her concern was about what people would say about me having a child with a disability. I was utterly shattered by Mum's reaction and by her comments about me tearing the family apart. However, my siblings completely accepted Emma, and with sheer joy.

Emma went to surgery at 8.15am on the Monday, just two days after she was born. Greg had come straight from the airport to the hospital in time to see Emma being wheeled off to surgery. He was exhausted from all the travel, so when Emma came out of surgery he went home to rest.

A few hours later I was brought to the ICU because Emma had crashed and had to be resuscitated. Medical staff advised me that because Emma had a disability they would not

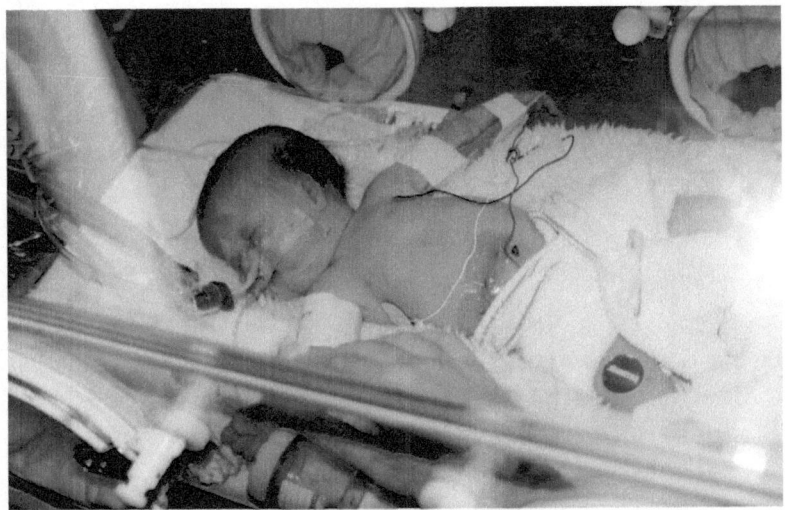

Our beautiful Emma, fighting to live

resuscitate her if she crashed again. I stayed in the ICU until I was given an assurance that she would receive whatever care she needed to survive. I wanted my daughter to live.

In the early hours of the morning after her surgery I sat beside her in ICU, gently talking to her about all kinds of things... from her brothers' names to describing her bedroom to letting her know how much I loved her and couldn't wait for her to come home. One of the doctors sat beside me and asked how I was doing. He then said, "Mrs Lynam, why don't you just go home and get on with your life. Leave her here. We will find somewhere to put her". I was shocked at this and could only shake my head. When I looked at my daughter I saw beauty and perfection. I couldn't understand what the doctors were seeing – clearly, not perfection.

That nurse in recovery had been right, though. There was a great deal to take in, including finding out that Emma also had a cleft palate.

When I was pregnant I looked forward to the arrival of my baby, just like any expectant mum. One of the things I most looked forward to was being able to breastfeed. Seeing friends and family breastfeeding their babies always felt like such a beautiful, miraculous thing. To me, the act of feeding a baby was like having a cord or bond between the mother and baby. When Roshan was a baby I had tried for a while to use a supply line so that we might have that miraculous connection. Unfortunately, at 12 weeks Roshan was a little too old and he wouldn't tolerate the slow rate at which the milk came through the tube. I hoped that this time, because I'd had a baby, I might be able to experience breastfeeding. But Emma's cleft palate made that impossible. The gaping hole in her palate meant she couldn't get a good enough seal on the nipple to be able to suck properly. I didn't have any trouble producing milk for her, but getting it into her was the problem. So for the first little while Emma was fed via a nasogastric tube.

Initially, I was told that I would have to learn how to tube Emma to be able to take her home. That seemed terrifying but, if that's what it took to be able to take Emma home then I would do it. Fortunately, the occupational therapist (OT) stepped in and suggested we try some different kinds of bottles and teats. We tried bottles with one-way valves and all kinds of teats. Nothing seemed to work. So I decided to try feeding Emma with a syringe. It was very slow-going. Getting 50ml into her would take about two hours.

The hospital had also stipulated that Emma's being able to go home would be determined by her weight and how well she was feeding. The challenge was that it took so long to feed her, she would get tired and fall asleep – this meant she was always down at least one feed and was therefore slow to gain weight.

After 10 days in hospital, I came home. Intellectually, I understood why Emma couldn't come home. But that day, as we drove away and left my precious little girl in the care of strangers, I was absolutely heartbroken. Upon arriving home I walked into her room, sat in the rocking chair, and cried. This beautiful room felt so wrong without her. I was utterly torn between the joy of being home with my boys and the constant ache, in every fibre of my being, to be with Emma.

I was expressing milk around the clock, and I clung desperately to the hope that when Emma's palate was repaired I would be able to breastfeed her. Each morning would see me at the kitchen table expressing. Then, I'd get breakfast for the boys, and quickly run down to the hospital with the milk. After dropping the boys at school I would go to the hospital to be with Emma. When she slept I would go home, do some laundry, tidy up and then head back to the hospital. I would pick up the boys after school and we would all go to the hospital for a little visit. After dinner I would go back with more breastmilk and feed Emma. Sometimes a nurse would call late at night to say Emma was awake and unsettled, and would ask if I could go down and settle her back to sleep.

One night, at about 11pm, one of the nurses rang to say Emma was very upset. I checked on the boys and asked my neighbour to watch out for them. When I arrived, I picked Emma up, held her close and swayed to the music that was playing (the nursing staff often had the radio on in the background). Just then, the song "We Gotta Get Out of This Place" came on. I started to sing it aloud and dance around with Emma in my arms. I said to Emma, "This is your mantra, baby girl. We gotta get out of this place".

One of the nurses picked up the baby she was feeding and began to sing with me. Only she was singing, "YOU gotta get out of this place!" Before long other nurses joined us and we were all laughing and singing along with the radio.

After two months in hospital Emma finally came home in the November.

One afternoon, while Emma was asleep, I sat at the table to write thank-you cards to those who had sent flowers and gifts. At some point, I stopped writing thank-you notes and began writing a poem. When I say I was writing a poem, what I mean is that my hand was holding the pen but something far greater than me was writing the poem. It just flowed in one natural easy draft. When I sat back and read it I felt so blessed and taken care of. It felt a little like the vision I had had of Emma in my meditation, as though someone was standing there beside me, showing me that it was all going to be fine – that this was all perfection at play.

An Angel at My Door

An angel came unheard to my door,
her gift left me standing in awe.
A tapestry she carefully unfolded,
a way to show how our lives are moulded.
Like a tapestry our lives
together are spun,
And ours, my dearest, has
only just begun.
I asked her: "This tapestry is
set by what plan?"
She answered: "Tis divinely laid,
not by woman or man".
I said, "To me the edging seems not right".
Her answer: "Tis not the edging
but your sight".
To watch the sun dance upon this
divine thread
is to know for sure there is so much ahead.
The colours on the loom are
vibrant and bright,
if I choose to see them in the right light.
The loom moves always in and out,
in and out,
raising the question: What is life all about?
Not for striving and achieving,
but for loving, giving and receiving.
Times I feel this loom I could shatter,
but part of me knows the tests
don't matter.
Which is the creator, the loom or the hand?
Together they work strand by strand.

So, my precious, before the
angel departed,
she made clear the message
that she started...
That together as the loom and thread
much happiness will you spread.

Joanne Lynam, 1994

CHAPTER 6

Digging for Resilience

"Often our greatest lessons are learned when we are standing at the very edge of what we think is impossible."

— *Joanne Lynam*

mma had only been at home for a couple of days when Greg had to go back to work. This was a very stressful time for the boys and me. We all struggled to adjust to the new reality, one in which so much of my time was taken up with just caring for Emma. This included medical appointments, but by far the most challenging thing was trying to get sufficient milk into her each day. Using the syringe was very slow because I had to slowly, carefully drip the syringe's milk into her mouth in time with her swallowing. When I got the timing wrong the milk would come back up through her nose, causing her much distress. I would then have to settle her down and try again.

Our precious family, Christmas 1994

While it was a number of months before I saw anything of my mum, Dad was a wonderful support and would come and help me at the drop of a hat.

One day he shared a story with me that explained why he was so upset and concerned for Emma's future. I remember telling him not to worry, that I knew Emma would have a great life. I had no idea where this sense of certainty came from. That day he told me a story that explained why he was so concerned.

When Dad was a kid he would sometimes wag school and go fishing with a mate of his. One particular morning Dad woke up and thought it would be a good day for fishing. So he hid up the back of his mate's place and waited for him to come out so that he could suggest they forget school and go fishing. Dad then got the shock of his life. His mate's parents came out to the car carrying a little boy who had (what Dad would later discover to be) Down syndrome. He said that they put him in the back of the car and covered him up. When his mate came out, Dad asked him who the little boy was. He was shocked to hear that the little boy was his mate's brother.

His mate said that nobody knew about him, and he asked Dad not to tell anyone. Dad had been to his mate's place many times and had never before seen the little boy with Down syndrome. His mate explained that whenever someone came to the house the family would hide him. My dad told me that many years after this, he learned that the local doctor would see patients with a disability at his home, not at the surgery. The reasoning behind this? It was so other patients wouldn't feel uncomfortable at the surgery.

The words of that nurse in recovery were now sinking in. There was a great deal ahead of me.

CHAPTER 7

Up to My Armpits in Alligators

*"You must give up the life you planned in order to have
the life that is waiting for you."*

— *Joseph Campbell*

hen Emma was three months of age, we were referred to Australian Hearing (now known as Hearing Australia) for testing. The results showed Emma had mixed hearing loss. She was fitted with hearing aids. Keeping them in her ears was an exercise in super creativity. I couldn't count the number of times I went back to get a new set of aids because Emma had thrown one out of the car window or they were otherwise nowhere to be found. She was very proficient at getting rid of them. Lesson one in creativity: keep car windows closed and the air-conditioning on. Lesson two: put a little headband around her ears to stop her pulling the aids out.

Feeding was a constant challenge. At one of the many hospital appointments, an OT suggested we try a bottle that was very soft and could be fitted with a really soft teat. This worked a lot better than regular bottles and teats. But Emma was a champion sleeper and would fall asleep within minutes of starting to feed. I would have to keep waking her up throughout each feed, which made it a marathon effort just to get something into her. This was a constant source of stress. I wanted Emma to have her palate surgery sooner rather than later, but this would only happen once she reached a certain weight.

An appointment was made for Emma to be seen by a cleft palate team. I had been doing a lot of reading about cleft palate surgery and its relationship with good speech outcomes. Everything I had read and been told by speech pathologists showed that the sooner the palate was repaired, the better chance it would give Emma for gaining speech.

However, this appointment would be the third time in those first few months of her life when I experienced the way many medical professionals devalue people with disabilities (the first had been the reluctance by medical staff to consider resuscitating her if she crashed again after surgery and the second had been when a doctor had suggested leaving Emma at the hospital and finding her a new home). The team consisted of a room full of specialists, but the surgeon did all the talking. He announced that because Emma had Down syndrome he didn't think there was any urgency for the repair to be done – he doubted it would make much difference. When I challenged his thinking about Emma's need for the surgery, and highlighted its link to good speech outcomes, he simply repeated himself. He didn't think it would make any difference to the final outcome for Emma. The quality of her life was clearly of no significance. Putting future speech issues aside, the cleft palate was continuing to make feeding extremely difficult, and traumatic for Emma (and me). But the thing to note here is that it was a *team* of specialists in the room. Not one of them said a word; they just nodded their agreement with the surgeon. Of the 10 men in that room, not one saw any value in Emma. They did not consider that she might have things to say and share one day.

At 11 months of age Emma's palate repair was done, though not by the cleft palate team. She recovered well, but no matter how much I tried, Emma was never able to suck properly. I stopped fretting about bottles and teats and started to use a sippy cup – this worked well, finally.

At about 12 months of age, Emma was referred to an ophthalmologist. This specialist had a very warm, caring manner. As I write, Emma is 26 years old and he remains her specialist. He diagnosed cataracts in both eyes. The right eye is the only one that has so far required surgery. The ophthalmologist referred us to a paediatric ophthalmologist – a colleague whom he felt had more paediatric experience. The day of this appointment is burned into my memory.

Our initial engagement with the paediatric ophthalmologist began in a pretty routine way – that is, until he read in Emma's notes that she had hearing loss and a cleft palate. "She is deaf and she has a cleft palate", he announced. "No shit, Sherlock!" I thought to myself. He said, "I think she might have Stickler syndrome". At the time all I could think was, "God, surely one syndrome is enough". He then suggested an appointment with a geneticist at a large public hospital. He made a time for the geneticist to see us later that day. Then, without a word to me, he picked up his phone and rang a colleague. This is how the conversation went: "Hi, Fred [not his real name] here. Look, I've got a little "downsie" here with mum, down from Townsville. I think the baby might have Stickler syndrome. I've got them going at

3 o'clock to see the geneticist. You've never seen that. Why don't you pop up there and have a look?" He then hung up and rang another colleague and said the same thing.

As I sat there in front of him I felt a sense of absolute rage rising in me. This feeling was new. He finally looked at Emma and said, "Now, where were we?" Next, without planning to, I heard myself say, "Organising a freak show, I think". He became flustered and mumbled an apology, to which I said, "Just get on with it so we can get out of here". He walked us to the reception, where he apologised again. As I headed for the door his receptionist said that I needed to pay the bill. I told her to send it. She advised me that if it wasn't paid at the time of the appointment it would incur a $30 fee. Now I was just plain angry. I looked at the doctor, who was standing there looking like a deer stuck in the headlights, and said, "If your time is worth $130 today, guess what? It's only worth that in 30 days". I left his bill on the table and paid the original amount at the 30-day mark and I didn't hear a word about it.

We went to the hospital that afternoon to see the geneticist (needless to say, the other doctors did not turn up for the "freak show"). She took one look at Emma and said, "Your daughter doesn't have Stickler syndrome". She then showed me photos of children with Stickler syndrome and explained that it is diagnosed by appearance. The paediatric specialist had got it wrong. I was so relieved.

Shortly after the challenging medical appointment with the paediatric ophthalmologist I formed a small playgroup with other mums, some of whom also had a child with a disability. The attitudes and insensitive behaviour of medical specialists was a topic that came up often in this little group. I spent considerable time coaching one mum on how to address their ill-thought-through remarks. I acknowledged that the specialists weren't bad people and that they weren't going out of their way to be deliberately hurtful. I felt they needed to step up and practise a little compassion and respect. After all, they were all making money out of children with disability.

I look back at my experience with the paediatric ophthalmologist as a great lesson because it gave me an opportunity to stand up and not take that kind of ill-informed, arrogant horseshit ever again. I didn't know it at the time but I was slowly gaining more awareness of my resilience.

In those very early days of Emma's life, when there were lots of appointments, it was hard on all of us. Roshan and Laksiri had to adjust to the new reality, one in which Emma was going to take a lot of my time away from them.

For a long time it was difficult for me to look back at that period and not feel sad and guilty. I felt guilt for all the occasions on which the boys missed out because so much of my time was going into Emma. However, I do also see that there were valuable lessons for all of us during that time.

A couple of years ago the boys came over to have dinner with me and we were talking about what life was like when Emma was little. I asked them if they felt that their childhoods were affected negatively by all the time given to Emma. Interestingly, neither of them felt that they had lost out on anything. In fact, they each felt they had gained a great deal because of Emma. At the time, there was a movie out that portrayed a person with an intellectual impairment. Roshan shared with me that his mates didn't "get" that movie. They thought it was lame. Roshan said he told them that it's different when you live that experience.

I now see that both of the boys are very caring and compassionate people as a result of the struggles they saw play out around Emma, and because they witnessed our efforts to create a normal life for her. Both of my beautiful sons show wisdom beyond their years. A couple of years back Laksiri and I were talking about what things we might need to be aware of for Emma in the future. Laksiri's insightful responses blew me away. I commented to him that I didn't have anything like that level of understanding at his age. He simply responded, "Sure, Mum, but you didn't have an Emma in your life".

CHAPTER 8

The Unopened Gifts

"It is my logical, rational mind that puts limits on what is possible."

— *Gerald G Jampolsky, MD*

By the time Emma was about a year old, I was once again involved with the local meditation centre and trying to undertake a daily meditation at home – this was an important part of keeping all of the balls in the air.

It was also about this time that I was introduced to *A Course in Miracles*, through a friend. My first thought was, "I don't think this is for me". I attended a study group for the course, and the leader suggested we all turn to the end of the course and read the epilogue. As we began to read the epilogue it felt as though an ancient door swung open within me. I had a strong inner sense of, somehow, having known this material before. That night was a turning point for me, and from that time on the epilogue's message has been an ongoing light in my life whenever I feel drawn to read it.

I couldn't stop the tears from flowing down my face. To this day the passage always touches me very deeply.

The epilogue's words felt as though they were calling to some long-lost part of me. A part of myself I would tap into occasionally, like the times when a poem would just roll out of me onto the page. Very often – sometimes for many years – I didn't even know what the poem was about. Like many people, I have worked with the *A Course in Miracles* teachings over a long time, but I have had breaks from it. Very often, when I feel as though I can't manage life anymore, something from the course will come to me. It always feels like a salve on a wound. The wound being, no doubt, my wounded pride. Whenever I open *A Course in Miracles* I always go to the epilogue and feel the comfort of its words. It often feels so new.

A great deal of what I was learning on my spiritual path I was applying to my life with Emma. I was constantly asking myself questions such as, "How would Emma experience meditation? Would it be as useful to her? How would I go about teaching or explaining it to her? Surely she, too, would benefit from meditation?"

One morning in meditation, I saw myself sitting in a circle with a group of people who were all quietly meditating – they each appeared to have some form of disability. Several had Down syndrome. After that, this vision visited me several times during my morning meditations. I didn't really know what these visions were about, or why I kept having them.

This was 1996. At that time in Australia most people born with a disability were still living in institutions where they were supposed to be cared for. There were several such institutions in Townsville. I had never been to any of these, nor did I know anyone in such a place.

One morning a few weeks later, as Emma and I sat peacefully in the rocking chair enjoying the early morning quiet, an idea gently, ever-so-quietly came to visit. It suggested I go to visit one of these institutions and ask about having a weekly get-together with some of the residents, for meditation or chanting. A moment of great doubt quickly shattered the peace of the early morning as my mind began to ask, "Who am I to think I could teach people with disability what meditation is and how it might be useful for them?"

Later that morning I rang one of the institutions and explained what I would like to try. To my amazement, management was very happy for me to come along and see how it went. I suggested that Emma and I could start off by coming for a few weeks at morning-tea time so people could get to know us.

Our first morning was an interesting mix of chaos, concern and joy. Emma was a big hit, with everyone wanting to hold her. It was a bit like "pass the parcel", with Emma being kissed and passed around. Staff were very concerned about Emma – but she wasn't concerned, so neither was I. As I sat in the midst of the large group of people I was acutely aware of being encircled by a wave of sheer love. I realised that I felt very at home and comfortable with this group of people with disability. For the next few weeks we just repeated this morning-tea and baby-holding routine.

I soon felt that the time was right to begin introducing meditation. I had absolutely no idea what was going to happen when we decided to run the first session. I didn't know what I was going to do or how I was going to do it. However, I trusted that I would be guided in the right direction. It was clear that the residents were comfortable with me and Emma, so that was a great start.

Management had suggested that we start the first session with all of us sitting on the floor in a little circle. We began with just eight people. I felt drawn to start with chanting. I had

*As I sat in the midst of
the large group of people
I was acutely aware of
being encircled by a wave
of sheer love.*

a CD with me, and I began playing the chant. I then closed my eyes and started to chant along with the CD, and the residents followed my lead. I never could have imagined the sheer bliss that I would feel in the company of this remarkable little group. One particular young man blew my heart open. After a few rounds of quietly listening to the chant, he started to join in with the others – and he had the voice of an angel. I opened my eyes to see who this angel was. I had been told earlier that this young man had autism and that he would be unable to chant because he was non-verbal.

He was no longer rocking backwards and forwards but was sitting perfectly still, in a crossed-legged position, chanting in time with the chant. Sure, his diction wasn't accurate, but the power that brought him to this earth, in this body, at this time, knew that he was chanting with all of his heart. When we finished our half-hour session he remained still and I quietly left the class. I was very curious to know how his week had gone, so at the start of the following week's session I asked staff. They mentioned that he had maintained that "stillness" for several hours. In that second session we went straight into the chant. This time, I watched to see what would happen. Again, he just listened for a while, and he then took in a big breath, straightened his spine and chanted like an angel.

Emma also very much enjoyed these sessions. She didn't chant, but as soon as the chanting began she would bum-shuffle over to me and sit on my lap, not moving until it was finished. She would then bum-shuffle around the circle to each person and give them a cuddle. These little sessions came to an end a few months after they started because the process of de-institutionalisation saw the residents move out (supposedly into community life). Many years later, when I was in a justice department role, I met up with some of them in various homes across the community.

My experiences with this little group set in motion a clear vision of "the power of possibility". As individuals, most of the time we don't know what we are capable of, so we surely can't decide what others are capable of.

I often felt that this little group of beautiful people were like Christmas gifts that had been left under the tree. Gifts that no one had bothered to unwrap.

CHAPTER 9

A Moment in Time

*"Enlightenment is as close to you as your own
most troubling thought."*

— *Byron Katie*

The challenges of my past followed me through all areas of my life, like a shadow. I felt that the rape I had experienced as a young musician was always near me, despite the passing of the years. I just wanted it to be gone, to be far away. In the years after the rape I was searching for some way to make peace with the pain. I guess you could say that my searching for peace drew me towards things of a spiritual nature.

It took me many years to realise that my constant seeking was a way of trying to ease the ever-present sense of fear and shame. Those feelings haunted my dreams at night and stalked me like a shadow throughout my days. The rape may have occurred years before, but it held onto me with a vice-like grip. Within me, the candle of fear and shame burned strongly. This nagging fear played out in the need to be right, the development of an eating disorder, the need to look my best, a concern about how others saw me, an overwhelming need for reassurance and a need to be vigilant.

I am very grateful to Greg, who never saw what I chose to see in myself at that time. I know I made his life very difficult. I love him all the more for his patience.

Not long after Greg and I were married, I started going to yoga classes. One night, I noticed a book the teacher had on the floor beside her. It was called *Autobiography of a Yogi* by Paramhansa Yogananda. This book became a lifeline for me, pulling me towards a different understanding of – and a greater appreciation for – the resilience that had helped me to keep looking for peace. I read it over and over, hoping that by just reading it I would become like the author. I wanted to experience the kind of bliss and non-attachment of which Yogananda spoke. I tried to meditate but didn't really grasp it.

Many years later, I was introduced to a very different form of meditation at a workshop. Through this workshop I was exposed to many wonderful spiritual understandings, all of which I have taken something from.

Joining my local meditation centre was just another step on this spiritual journey. Here again I was reading and experiencing a new level of spirituality. My trip to the ashram was another step in my inward journey.

Sometime in the late '90s, I read a book in which there was a little story. This tiny story changed my life forever. It went something like this: a little new soul met a much older soul and the older soul spoke of forgiveness. And the little soul wanted to know about forgiveness. So it was agreed that the old soul would go down to earth with the little soul to give the little soul an opportunity to forgive. Just as the old soul and the little soul were about to depart for earth, the old soul turned to the little soul and said, "When I come to you and I do something so horrible to you, will you remember me?"

As I read those words, it felt as though a dam had burst within me. I was sobbing uncontrollably because, in that very moment, I KNEW that the rape had been what I had long ago "agreed to". I knew that the three men had each agreed to play their parts as the rapists and I would play the part of the victim – until I remembered who I really was. As strange as it may sound, in that moment I forgave those three men and acknowledged that they had simply played their part.

I had started that day with the shadow of the rape still hanging over me. But that night I went to bed without the shadow. The experience of reading those words – "Will you remember me?" – was profound because, in that single moment, forgiveness happened and I was no longer living under the shadow of the rape. I was free.

From that moment, I no longer saw myself as a victim or as a survivor; rather, I saw myself as an actor in the stage play called life. This is not to say that I have forgotten the rape or that it doesn't come to the surface from time to time; it does. But it no longer tortures me. It serves as a reminder that I am greater than my earthly experiences; they are just lessons I have agreed upon.

This profound experience also offered me a very clear real-isation that, while I had lived in fear for a long time, I had also been developing an inner strength or resilience. That inner strength was there to guide me through Laksiri's adoption and its enormous emotional toll. It was also there through the early days with Emma. I give thanks every day for my resilience. I now know that it is the greatest part of me. It is the presence of something profound in me, as it is in all of us.

I am not defined by what happened in one moment of time; rather, I am able to choose how I define myself, *despite* that one moment in time.

Hidden Talents

"Why fit in when you were born to stand out?"

— *Dr Seuss*

Right from the beginning, Emma showed us that she was wicked-smart in a devious kind of way. She was definitely no pushover. Despite having an army of volunteers coming to the house five days a week to do cross-crawl patterning with her, she never did crawl. But that's not to say that she wasn't mobile – she surely was. Emma does things in her own way. She would shuffle around on her bum and could get up quite a speed when she wanted to. At this time Emma was a bit like a bower bird, looking for shiny interesting things in her brothers' rooms. It was always easy for the boys to find what she had taken because everything went back to her room (the nest).

When Laksiri was a bit older he moved into the down-stairs bedroom, no doubt thinking he would be safe from his sticky-beak little sister. His fish tank was his pride and joy, and Emma was fascinated with it. She just loved to throw all manner of things into it.

Every now and then Emma would have a fashion parade, of sorts... with everyone else's clothes. Dad's size 11 shoes, my T-shirt, Roshan's cap and Laksiri's "good pants" – down the hallway she would come shuffling on her little bum, as fast as she could.

Even at this early stage in her life Emma was a great mimic. She could do a fantastic impersonation of my mum. Whenever Mum came to the house Emma would put her hands on her hips, clap her hands and wag her finger at Mum. This is exactly what Mum used to do to Emma. Mum wasn't amused, but the rest of us thought it was hysterical and would crack up laughing. Similarly, whenever Emma did something that was a bit cheeky or mischievous, my dad would punch his right fist into his left palm and say to Emma, "I'll put you on the knuckle!" Emma would laugh and shuffle off. One day Dad came for a visit, and as soon as Emma saw him she made a fist and punched it into her hand. She then laughed and shuffled off. This was a very good indication that Emma knew exactly what was going on with Dad – she got the joke and was giving it back to him. Dad just loved it.

I recall trying to use her mimicking skills to her benefit, to encourage her to wear her glasses and hearing aids. Emma had several teddies and dolls at the time. I got hold of some old reading glasses and put them on the teddies and dolls to show Emma that they were just like her. When Emma didn't want to put on her glasses I would show her that teddy and dolly were wearing their glasses. Of course, Emma is a pretty smart little cookie and it didn't take long for her to figure out what I was doing. She would take the glasses off the teddy and dolls, look at me, and sign, "Same me".

Emma, age 3, with her bespectacled teddy & dollies

When Emma was about three or four years of age, she no longer slept through the evening program when I took her with me to the local meditation centre. I was part of the musical team on those evenings, playing the drum to accompany the harmonium and bells. Each week Emma would begin the night sitting beside me. But, once the chant started and was swinging along, Emma would become a little pickpocket. Bum-shuffling from handbag to handbag, she would remove anything she liked the look of – lipstick, purses, photos – and then shuffle back to me and leave all of her booty beside me. At the end of the night, people would gather up their things, and fortunately they saw the funny side of Emma's antics. I was often reminded of the song "You've Got to Pick a Pocket or Two".

When she was a little older she figured out that Laksiri liked to have the weekly TV guide at his fingertips. I could not count the number of times when she would be casually playing, or watching something on TV, and she would spot the "unguarded" TV guide. I would watch her take it and hide it down the side of the lounge chair or under one of the chair's cushions. Several hours later Laksiri would be looking for the TV guide and Emma would just sit there on the couch, looking completely innocent. The best part was when Laksiri would ask her if she knew where the guide was. She would shrug her shoulders and sign, "I don't know". Then, when Laksiri left the room, she would produce the guide.

Emma was also a grand master at sizing up therapists and trying to get out of engaging in anything she didn't like the look of. In the end, Emma would find her own unique ways of doing things (usually to the disgust of her therapists). She was well behind her peers, developmentally – the simple act of going from lying to sitting was a challenge for her. One day during a physio appointment I explained that Emma could now sit up by herself. I put Emma on the floor on her tummy, and she took her legs straight out to the side of her body, using her arms to push herself to sitting position. Needless to say, the physio was not impressed. She said, "That's not the way you are supposed to sit up, Emma". She tried numerous times to have Emma cross her legs when she made it upright but Em, being Em, wasn't having a bar of that.

Walking was another area in which Emma was well behind her peers. Having a foot deformity meant that it was difficult for her to get her balance. The physiotherapist arranged for her to be fitted for a standing frame. This would help her begin to bear weight, which was a first step towards her being able to eventually walk. However, at the time, I am quite sure that Emma thought something along the lines of, "There is no need to worry about walking because Mum is perfectly capable of carrying me. That is, after all, my pre-ferred way of getting around!"

We also had a regular appointment with an OT. She was a very experienced woman but her methods for getting Emma to do things, such as holding a pencil, proved to be unhelp-ful. Instead of trying to encourage Emma through praise or rewards, she would force Emma's fingers around a pencil and then tape them in place. While this was well-meaning, it was clear to me that this was not the way to win over Emma. In the end, Emma would cry as soon as we walked into the OT's office. I tried to encourage her by praising any little effort that she made towards holding a pencil or crayon. I gave her rewards and sought out grip devices that could be put onto pencils or crayons – while the grips definitely helped, Emma still struggled. I look back and can see that Emma probably wondered what was the purpose of trying to hold a pencil or crayon. Perhaps she would have been more interested if she had been shown why it was a good thing.

At around this time Emma and I joined a signing playgroup. All the mums were deaf and had hearing children. I thought it might help my signing skills to be around people who signed. I also knew that it would be of great benefit to Emma to be around more people who were using sign language. I had no idea what I was in for with this group of women. They were all signing at a breakneck speed and I found myself constantly signing, "I am sorry – can you repeat that for me?" The mums were so patient and genuinely wanted to help me. They never seemed to mind repeating things for me.

However, with these lovely ladies I learned a great deal more than just signing. They were some of the most perceptive people I have ever met. Their ability to read people was uncanny. Let me explain. One day I turned up for playgroup having come from a very challenging medical appointment. I felt upset and angry, but as I drove to the playgroup I regrouped and put on my game face – at least, that's what I thought I had done. The moment I walked into the room, the mums were straight onto me, asking me questions. They knew that I was far from fine. I saw this kind of thing so often with these remarkable ladies.

They also had a fabulous sense of humour. One night we all went out for a meal at a local restaurant. At the end of the meal a young waiter came and asked if we would like tea or coffee. Most of the ladies simply wrote down for the waiter what they wanted. But Sue (not her real name) sitting beside me decided to sign the word "coffee". He took a guess on it being coffee, and was thrilled that he got it right. My friend winked at me as he asked her if she wanted her coffee to be white or black. Sue looked at him and took hold of her breast, as if to squeeze milk from it. The poor young waiter went a deep shade of red, but he understood and laughed.

My time with the signing playgroup was a very beautiful experience that I looked forward to each week. Some of these ladies shared stories of their experiences of growing up deaf and the awful ways in which they had been treated, particularly at school. A number of them were sent away to deaf school at a very young age. I could only marvel at their

They were some of the most perceptive people I have ever met. Their ability to read people was uncanny.

willingness to forgive and move on. Sue had done a hair-dressing apprenticeship in a very busy salon. As a profoundly deaf woman, she must have worked twice as hard as every other hairdresser in the salon because she had to use all of her senses to read customers' lips and body language. Sue's success, against the odds, reveals what can happen if we focus on possibility. Her resilience is also something we can all access within ourselves, if we are willing to trust that it is there for us.

Emma got her sign name from these beautiful ladies. As I mentioned earlier, at that time Emma was very happy to be carried everywhere on my hip. One day, Sue commented that Emma was always snuggled up to me like a koala. So, there and then, Emma was given her sign name: "Koala". If you head to Emma's page on my website – joannelynam .com.au/emma – you can watch a video of Emma signing this name.

CHAPTER 11

Closed Doors

"There are things known and there are things unknown, and in between are the doors of perception."

— *Aldous Huxley*

The year Emma was born was Roshan's last year of primary school. Roshan would be moving on to high school the next year. While I knew Roshan wanted to attend the same high school as many of his friends, getting the boys to two different schools in different parts of the city would have been just too stressful for all concerned. So we put both boys into a combined primary and secondary school very close to our home.

One day just before the school year ended, I spoke with Roshan's principal about Emma and her schooling. He was very clear that getting Emma into a faith-based school would be very difficult. As I drove away from the school it felt as though I was watching a slow-motion movie. Different moments of time, from Emma's birth onwards, slowly flashed before me. Things such as the way people looked at Emma, the way some families at the school had avoided me, the nurse at the hospital who had told me that I had a long, hard road ahead of me... It occurred to me in that moment that I hadn't seen any children at the school with a disability. Where were they? My mind went back to my own days at school. Why hadn't I seen anyone like Emma at school? Why didn't I see people like Emma shopping, or in the park?

Then, I had a crystal-clear memory of a day in the ashram in India. I was sitting just outside the temple because it was very crowded. I had looked up as a group of the local village children were walking past the temple. A little boy of about five years of age stopped right in front of me. He looked at me for a long time and smiled. He had Down syndrome. As my mind went back to that day, a calm feeling washed over me. I realised this was another reminder that everything is unfolding as it is intended.

I could also hear my words to the nurse in recovery: "This little girl is not going to be hidden away; you are going to know about her".

The Aldous Huxley quote at the beginning of this chapter tells us, "There are things known and there are things unknown, and in between are the doors of perception". I wondered a great deal at the time whether or not the "suits" within education ever thought about the way they were looking at things. Perhaps they were just so sure that they were on the side of right? I also wondered if they had ever opened the doors of perception.

At this point, one thing was clear to me. To get Emma into a mainstream school I was going to need all the strength and resilience I had.

CHAPTER 12

Patience Is a Gift

*"Inclusion is being valued for who you are, as you are.
It is being asked to sit at the table, and knowing
you belong at the table — true inclusion also means
your contributions are appreciated and your gifts and
talents are recognised as valuable."*

— Joanne Lynam

Shortly after the boys started at their new school I went to talk to the school's primary principal.

Firstly, I wanted to get to know him. Secondly, I wanted to sound him out about Emma attending the school. He seemed warm and friendly and he didn't say, "No, Emma can't come to the school". So I hoped all would be well.

Not long after, the school announced that there would be a meeting to discuss with families the future plans for the school. I thought this sounded good. Surely the subject of students with a disability would be a part of their future planning, right?

However, the focus of the meeting was on expansion and infrastructure, including where resources would need to go in the future. The formal part of the meeting finished and it was then open for questions. By this stage, I was thinking, "Why haven't they discussed plans for students with disability?" A number of parents had their hands up to ask questions so I waited to see if any questions would relate to the inclusion of students with disabilities. There were none, so I raised my hand and said, "I note that this meeting is about future planning, so I am wondering when you might say something in regard to students with disabilities". A mother behind me yelled out, "The government's got places for kids like that and it's not here". I was told that this was not the time or the place for that kind of question. So I asked when would be the right time and place. The meeting was immediately ended. It is the saddest thing to me that one mother can cast out another's child and not see that in doing so she wounds her own child just as much.

So the rose-coloured glasses were now off.

A few weeks later the school had a welcome night for new families and we were invited. There was a welcoming team made up of parents from the school committee. Imagine my joy to find that the mother who had yelled out at the future-planning meeting was part of the welcoming team. The team parted like the Red Sea as we walked up. We found a table and sat down. While all of the other tables had a number of families talking and being welcomed, we were left – a family of five at a table for 10 – on our own. No one from the welcoming team came near us.

By the time Emma was four she was going to a regular playgroup. Emma really enjoyed all aspects of playgroup, and fingerpaint and Play-Doh were her favourite activities. She was getting much better with her glasses and hearing aids by this time and I only had to go on treasure hunts through the house a couple of times a week to look for them. However, I do recall turning the playground upside down one afternoon at the end of playgroup, trying to find yet another pair of hearing aids.

Very early in Emma's life we committed to learning to sign so that we could communicate with her. Every day I would place Emma in her highchair for her lunch. As I did so, I would sign, "Eating lunch" to her and then sign the question, "Do you want a drink?" Many months went by without Emma giving any indication that she understood or was going to sign. One day, though, I went through the usual motions of signing to her and beginning to prepare her lunch. I looked up at her, and she smiled at me. Then she clearly signed, "Eating" and "Drink". I swept her up out of the highchair and hugged her. I cried with absolute joy, as it clearly meant she understood – and this meant there was a way forward.

I began to work with Emma every day, reading and signing to her from a wide range of children's books. She was a good student and quick learner. Very soon she could sign entire small-children's stories. She was also picking up signs for all kinds of things. One afternoon I asked Dad to come over to help me. When he arrived I sat Emma on my lap with one of her favourite books, and showed Dad how she was learning to sign animals, colours and objects in the book. Dad was very emotional as he watched Emma signing her way through a little book. He cried and kept saying, "Oh, Jo, she understands! That's wonderful".

When Emma was engaged in social activities like playgroup, her signing was very helpful. If little children are not tainted by adults around them, they are very open to new experiences. Learning a "secret language" that Mummy and Daddy didn't know was a lot of fun for the other children. Each week at playgroup children would ask me to show them new signs, which I was only too happy to do. It was just delightful to watch them quickly grasp a new sign and then run off to show their mum or dad. When we had singing at playgroup I would sit beside Emma and sing and sign to her. Slowly, she began to join in, as did the other children. I loved the way children would be singing along and then suddenly throw in a few of the signs that they knew well. All of this was very good for Emma as – without any effort or special attention – she was hearing normal speech patterns, and the natural play of children was being modelled for her. She was also picking up on the excitement of the other children at learning new signs. This greatly encouraged her to want to sign more.

When Emma had her hearing aids in, it was clear that she really enjoyed music. We joined a small music group. However, at this time there was still a lot of resistance to having a person with a disability included in any kind of regular setting. Each week I could feel the very closed-off energy from the other mothers in this group. It didn't seem to matter how friendly I was; they never wanted to talk or, for the most part, make eye contact with me. At the end of class one day, one of the mums handed a pile of birthday invitations to the teacher to give to the children. The teacher called each child's name and handed them their invitation. There was no invitation for Emma. The following week, the mum in question explained that she didn't know if Emma would be able to go to a birthday party, which is why she hadn't given her an invitation. I made the choice to simply nod at her. I was beginning to see that the road to inclusion was rough and barren.

During this time I was speaking with the primary principal on a regular basis regarding how we might go about getting Emma into school. He was always polite and friendly but made no commitment. The following year Emma went to kindergarten, where she settled in easily and the staff were lovely and accepting. However, I was also made aware that not all the parents shared the teachers' inclusive mindset.

When Emma was first diagnosed with hearing loss I started reading everything I could get my hands on about speech development and language. My reading revealed that Emma would need some means to communicate. I made the decision to learn to sign, so that I could teach this to Emma. The research showed that it didn't really matter how you got language into a child – whether it be via speech, sign language or a communication device. What mattered was that the child had a way of clearly communicating. We had no internet then, so I relied on OTs and speechies (speech pathologists) to guide me towards helpful information. I would find the recommended research through the library and have it copied or sent to me.

During her year in kindy it was particularly gratifying to see Emma copying what the other children were doing. Her ability to mimic or copy is a great strength. By watching the other children and copying them, she was learning new skills. These included skills such as how to use a shovel in the sandpit, and how to use cookie cutters to make Play-Doh shapes. One day I watched a little girl patiently try to show Emma how to draw. The little girl didn't attempt to explain anything; she just demonstrated what to do and Emma did her best to follow. I couldn't help but think that this little girl had done more to help Emma with the skill of holding a pencil than the OT ever did. From my point of view it was all really wonderful to see Emma learning, just by watching. To this day she learns best if she is allowed to take her time and just watch and copy. The staff were very open to having her in the group and they encouraged all of the children to use sign language because they felt it would be good for their development. However, I was painfully aware that not all parents shared that view.

Emma also copied a lot of other things children did, including their not-so-great behaviour. Once there was a little girl throwing a real tantrum in the kindy's home corner. She was crying, and yelling, "I want it! I want it!" and banging the side of the playhouse. Emma was intrigued. She went over to the playhouse and started banging the side of it in the same way. The little girl throwing the tantrum immediately stopped and looked at Emma. Her tantrum finished right there. The funny thing was, later that afternoon Emma and her brothers were watching a DVD when, out of the blue, Emma started banging on the coffee table. When I saw her doing this I knew she was just having another go at what she had seen the little girl do. By watching the little tantrum-thrower, Emma had learned how to get the attention of others. She was simply trying that out with her brothers. Their instant reaction showed Emma that it worked. I always felt that Emma's ability to copy others said a great deal about her ABILITY, not her disability. She became so good at learning this way that you had to be careful that she didn't pick up things you don't want her to know – such as how to operate the TV remote!

CHAPTER 13

Beyond the Walls

"Strength doesn't come from what you can do. It comes from
overcoming the things you once thought you couldn't."

— *Rikki Rogers*

I n the late '90s in Queensland, the education department was not particularly supportive of children with a
disability being included in public-school classrooms.
Fortunately for us, there had been many courageous and
persistent families who had walked the road ahead of us.
They paved the way for us to have more success in being
heard and valued. The same cannot be said for the faith-
based schools. The private and faith-based schools seemed
to have an air of entitlement, superiority and privilege. The
state system would accommodate children with disabilities, but they had a very strict policy stipulating that these
children had to go to their nearest state school. Officials
would take out a ruler and measure the distance on a map
between your home and the schools in your area. This was

to ascertain which school was the closest to you. However, the closest school might not have been able to provide the support that your child needed.

So when I was dealing with the department, out came the ruler to show me where the nearest state school was. It was only 400m from our home. I mentioned to the education department representative that I was actually planning on sending Emma to the same school as her brothers; he just smiled gently and said, "That will be difficult, but I wish you well".

We were very keen for Emma to go to preschool at this school and then to progress to year one – it would be a support to Emma to have the boys nearby, and the school was close to home. However, getting in was going to be the big challenge.

In the last few months of kindy, in the lead-up to preschool, Emma had a hearing advisory support teacher provided by the state system. She was very experienced and a wonderful advocate for Emma. With the benefit of 20/20 hindsight, I have no doubt that she knew the school would put up a lot of resistance to Emma being enrolled there. I had many meetings with the primary principal, but in the end he was a lot like Pontius Pilate – he washed his hands of us and passed us on to the head principal.

The advisory teacher had arranged a meeting for us with the head principal. I felt that because the head was a female, she would be more understanding. Big mistake! In the meeting, the advisory teacher and I were seated on one side of the table, and a number of "suits" from administration were on the other side. At the head of the table was the head principal, but she sat with her body turned away from our side of the table. Her legs were crossed, and she was swinging one of her legs. She had to look over her shoulder to make eye contact with me. Her body language spoke volumes. She made some noise about how much she would love to open the doors to all children, including those with a disability, but it posed great difficulty for them.

The advisory teacher explained that Emma would have her own aide in the classroom. This aide was funded by the state government. At the time of the meeting with the principal, Emma was still not able to walk. This was due to her foot deformity. The principal had tried to use this as a reason to prevent Emma from attending preschool. But the preschool teacher couldn't see a problem with Emma being in the group. In the end, Emma was allowed to attend preschool at the same school as her brothers.

Emma had a wonderful year at preschool – she engaged, and enjoyed it all. By the end of the year she was walking. As with kindy, by just being around other children she learned a great deal. The children in this group were all keen to help her walk. They would help her up onto her feet and say things like, "Come on, Emma! You can walk".

In the early days at preschool we began trialling some of the communication devices that were coming onto the market. Speak Easy was one. Although it was a lot of work to record all of the commands onto it, it meant that Emma had an opportunity to engage in show and tell, and to share her life with the other children. At that age children are like little sponges, absorbing everything. They have no concept of disability or difference. In fact, most of the children were very curious about how Emma's communication device worked. Once I showed them how to use it, they took over recording what Emma had done that day at preschool. I felt a great sense of joy and satisfaction about that. If only children were the ones making the decisions about who came to the school...

While Emma was having fun at preschool I was in meetings with the school about her starting year one the following year. At that time, the education department had an assessment

*At that age children
are like little sponges,
absorbing everything.
They have no concept of
disability or difference.*

system for all children with a disability. It worked like this: department "experts" would go through all the assessments that had been done on your child, allocate a number to their physical, intellectual, visual and auditory abilities, and then decide on the level of support your child would need. This all sounds good, in theory. In reality, it was all about how much aid time your child could get. It was like throwing out scraps of funding for the begging families to fight over.

I felt outraged about the way in which the assessments had been done – in particular, the very unfair way in which the speech pathologist had carried out the assessment of Emma's communication. The speech pathologist didn't use sign, and she had said all along that she felt signing to Emma was a mistake. On the day of the assessment she produced books that featured animals not from Australia, but from the northern hemisphere (eg, skunks, squirrels and moose). Emma had never seen these animals so she didn't know the signs. In fact, I didn't know the signs for them. I was incensed. This part of the assessment had been done in such an unfair and unjust way.

The IQ test was structured in a similar way, with items and pictures that Emma wasn't able to explain. It was believed that if a person can't speak, then they don't understand. Even at that early stage I knew Emma understood a great deal of what was going on around her but she just couldn't say it. So, what is communication? Is it just the words we utter? Isn't watching, feeling, listening and body language also communication? I am sure you have had the experience of walking into a room of people and feeling either comfortable or uneasy before you have even met or spoken to anyone. We have all had the experience of meeting someone for the first time and feeling an instant connection with them, despite there being very little verbal communication. Aren't we watching and feeling the communication in these situations? Aren't these communications indicative of understanding?

The next step in this process (the process of ensuring that each child was completely devalued and their parents were trampled into the dust) was the ascertainment meeting. Parents were invited to be part of this meeting. It was at this stage that your child was given the number that indicated the level of support they would require – the higher the number, the greater the level of support. You might think that I would have wanted that number to be a six, the highest. But I didn't. This is because the school administrators had told me, at a previous meeting, that if Emma was determined to be a six she would not be able to attend the school.

The advisory teacher had said she would come with me to the ascertainment meeting, for support. At 8.30am one day the advisory teacher called to advise that the school had made the arrangements for the meeting to be done via phone, at the school. The meeting was at 10am that day. I had no time to plan or to gather my thoughts about how I would handle this meeting. I knew that this was all part of the school's strategy – they wanted to ensure that I didn't have time to plan or to organise support. I was sure that even if this didn't stop me, they would cite a legislative loophole that said a school didn't have to take a child with a disability if it was deemed to cause undue hardship to the school.

I got to the school and was met by six suits from the school's administration, including the primary-school prin-cipal. They sat on the other side of the table. Because of the very short notice, the advisory teacher couldn't make it. I was on my own. The imbalance of power in the room was not lost on me. I had a strong feeling that it had been set up this way to try to intimidate me. Not a chance.

The education department was on the phone, and was pushing for a level six. They were citing Emma's intellectual impairment, hearing loss and lack of communication as the reason. I pushed back hard, but the department, not know-ing what was going on in the room, argued that Emma would need a level six for adequate support, and they then finished the call. The moment the call ended, the six suits stood up and the principal said, "Well, that's that. She is a six. As we have said before, we cannot support a level six child".

I then heard myself say, "Not so fast, gentlemen. I am not finished". They sat back down. I heard myself begin to talk to them about Mother Teresa of Calcutta. I then asked them a question: "Do you think that the first time Mother Teresa saw a beggar dying on the street that she said, 'I would really like to help you but I will have to check with Rome to ask if they will fund this'? No, she just picked up that man and carried him home. She did what she knew was the right thing to do. Money and assessments didn't come into it; she just did it". I then stood up and walked out the door.

I had watched and heard myself say things over which I had no control or cognitive awareness – it felt like an out-of-body experience. Something far greater than me or my personality was at work that day. I drove home with an incredible feeling of gratitude. Sure, I hadn't come out of the meeting with a winning hand. But the experience of being out of my body while something else took over filled me with peace. I knew I was being taken care of and everything would work out just as it was supposed to. Shortly after this meeting, a new head principal took over – by this time I knew within myself that I WOULD NOT QUIT, and I saw that I had the potential for a different outcome with the new principal. I spent a considerable amount of time with him, trying to help him see the benefits to the whole school community of including students like Emma. I pointed out that she would be able to teach tolerance, patience and compassion, and to demonstrate resilience.

On the very last day of preschool, at 3pm, the head principal asked me to come to the office. He introduced me to a woman who was a year one teacher, and he said that she had agreed to take Emma. I said hello and shook her hand. She then said, "Well, you're lucky I am here because nobody else wants her". Can you imagine? This was said in front of the school principal and he made no comment. How powerful they must have thought they were, entitled to push away anyone in whom they saw no value. As far as I was concerned, their attitude and behaviour reflected their fears about including someone different. Separation is the primary teaching of fear.

The teacher's comment concerned me. However, I felt that, with time and support, she and the school community would come around. How wrong I was.

The teacher, Mary (not her real name), and I agreed that for the first day of school it would be best to have Emma arrive a little after the rest of the class. This would make it a little easier for all concerned. My thinking was that sometimes the first day of school is upsetting for some children and their parents. I wanted Emma's first day of school to be a good memory for her, not one of upset and confusion at seeing other children crying.

While I was walking Emma to the classroom on her first morning, I heard the principal welcoming a family to the school. The parent said to the principal, "I am not happy about my daughter being in a class with some disabled kid. The government has places for kids like that". I took a deep breath and, in that precise moment, a line from *A Course in Miracles* came to grace me with patience: "Fearful people can be vicious". I silently said, "Thank you".

I did everything in my power to support Mary because, although she had been teaching for many years, she had never taught a child with a disability. I kept telling myself, "This is a good person. She is willing to give Emma a go". Greg and I paid for her to learn to sign. We sent her to Brisbane to do training with the Down Syndrome Association. I brought in Australian Hearing to talk to her and the students about hearing aids. The only informed and qualified special needs person coming into the class to truly support Emma was the government-provided advisory teacher. In this kind of non-government-school setting the role of her advisory teacher was to support the teacher in lesson planning and to spend time in the classroom with Emma (observing engagement and providing the teacher with feedback). She would show the teacher how to modify lessons for Emma so that she could be included but work at a level that she could manage. For example, when the class was learning to write words and sentences, Emma might have been learning to recognise the letters of the alphabet and how to sign them. In this way she would be working at her pace and still be included. Having children with a disability included in this way offers a powerful lesson to the other children in the class – it demonstrates that, with the right support, we are all able to learn and to achieve goals.

I spent a lot of time in the classroom with Emma. This was often not by choice. Rather, the teacher demanded that I be present if and when the class went anywhere.

I couldn't count the number of times children in the class came out with the most appalling comments. I knew these had come straight from their parents' mouths. I would be tying a child's shoelaces and they would say, "Mum says Emma is wasting her time here" or, "She is never going to be able to learn anything". Or they would say, "Dad says she shouldn't be here" or, "Dad said he's not paying fees for me to learn to sign". But I kept telling myself that it was just a matter of holding on, and that, in time, the school community would come to see the value of Emma.

The most difficult part of Emma's time in this class was the constant negative attitude of the teacher herself. On a fairly regular basis she would openly say to me, "Well, she's been bad all day. She's done no work" and she would just leave Emma at the back of the room. One afternoon the teacher asked me this question: "What's your plan here for

Emma, Jo? Because I can tell you that no one wants to take her in year two". I knew that this was correct because other teachers would look straight through me and Emma, as though we just weren't there. I sensed their hostility. Clearly, my wanting Emma to be included made these teachers fearful. I can't be sure of why they were so fearful of a little girl. Perhaps they doubted their own ability to support Emma, or perhaps they feared that they might look bad if it didn't go well. Or perhaps they were fearful that they would have to get out of their comfort zone and work differently to include Emma. By listening to the voice of fear, they missed an opportunity to help the entire school community take a journey of discovery – a journey showing that all new or different paths can open us to experiences we might never have dreamed possible.

Imagine a classroom where a child is sitting beside Emma (or any child like Emma). What is the child sitting beside the student with a disability learning, besides the curriculum? They are learning tolerance, empathy and patience. These are not things you can teach as a lesson; they are learned through experience. Now consider that, one day, the year-one student who sat beside a child with a disability goes on to become a leader, perhaps even a prime minister. Imagine a world where leaders make decisions through the lens of tolerance, empathy and patience, which they learned in year one by sitting beside a person with a disability.

One Friday, halfway through the year, I came to pick up Emma and discovered that she was sitting on the "naughty chair". This had happened before, but this time she was crying and signing, "Me bad, me bad" to me as I stood at the door. She signed to me that she had not come down from the play equipment when the teacher had asked her to, and the teacher had become angry. She had told Emma in front of the class that she was a very naughty girl, and she had then put her on the naughty chair. As soon as Emma shared

Imagine a world where leaders make decisions through the lens of tolerance, empathy and patience, which they learned in year one by sitting beside a person with a disability.

this with me, I knew that this environment was toxic and wrong for any child. I didn't bother waiting for the teacher to say that parents could come in. I just went straight to Emma and held her tight. I told her over and over again, "You are good, you are my beautiful girl, you are good".

I was heartbroken but, at the same time, I had a very clear focus on what needed to happen. I knew I had to get Emma out of there. I phoned the head of the education department to make plans for Emma to move to the state system. I remember saying to him, "Well, you were right, the non-government system didn't work". He was very supportive and put in place plans for Emma to move to a state school.

What I learned from this period is that although I had worked hard to win the battle with the "powers that be" at the school, I hadn't won their hearts and minds. I hadn't succeeded in helping them come to see the value of Emma to the whole school community. Was there something else I could have done? Or could I have done things differently? Perhaps it was just the wrong time and place. This very challenging time gave me a first-hand experience of what *A Course in Miracles* says about there being only two emotions – love or fear. Fear was very much at work within the administration and many families of this school.

Now, many years later, with the benefit of hindsight, it's clear to me that there are three groups of people. The first group have open minds and willing hearts, so they will always be able to walk in another's shoes. The second group may be closed-minded to begin with, but with information and support they can and will change their minds. The third group will never change their minds, no matter how much time and energy is put into them. With this group you have to just walk away – if you stay in that environment it will only lead to harm.

I have been asked whether or not I regret all the time and energy I put into pushing back against the closed doors of the "suits" and the hierarchy who, in my opinion, behaved so badly. I have no regrets about the manner in which I conducted myself, or about the time and energy I put into trying to have Emma accepted into "mainstream" education. My reason for pushing back against this kind of discrimination was exactly the same as when my son Laksiri came up against racism at school. My question is: if I hadn't pushed back and called out this kind of behaviour for the racism and discrimination that it was, what kind of message would I be sending to my children? If I just sat by and said and did nothing I would have been telling my sons and daughter, "Oh, it doesn't matter that people speak to you like this, just ignore it". No, that would be telling my children that this is what you can expect, that your place in life is accepting the crumbs that fall from the table of the privileged. Hell, no!

The problem lies in our human condition, where we separate ourselves based on our skin colour, religion, gender, sexuality or ability. We look first for difference and make that difference wrong and threatening. But the divine intelligence that beats in my heart and yours also beats in the heart of a person with a disability or with different skin, or a different gender. The Divine intended for them to be here just as they are. Therefore, it's up to us all to help each member of our human family find a purpose. In so doing, all our lives have a greater purpose because we have helped to raise the consciousness of our community. A community or country with an elevated level of consciousness can and will achieve great things.

Right now, if we look at OUR world, we see separation everywhere we look. We hold our separation so tightly to our chests like a coat of armour. We are unable to see that that coat of armour is suffocating us and our planet. Our separation is putting our planet and ALL its species in peril. We cannot live without the gift of water or clean air gifted to us by our planet. But our separation is blinding us to the very damage we are doing to the air and water. All living things on this planet are made up of the same elements as us; they are just arranged one way as a tree, a different way as a bird and another as a human. We all come from the same essence but our separation is killing not only us but the entire planet – our life-support system.

Imagine, if you will, the cells of your brain issuing a decree that they and they alone are the most powerful and important cells in the body. That skin cells and the cells of other organs are of less importance than the cells of the brain. The brain cells then begin to establish barriers and cut all communication with other cells. Without coherence and communication among the cells of the human body, it would quickly fail and die. All people, regardless of their colour, creed, sexuality or ability are like individual cells in the body of humanity. Just like the human body, our body of humanity needs all its parts working together in balance and harmony.

CHAPTER 14

Passion & Pain

"A nation should not be judged by how it treats its highest citizens, but its lowest ones."

— *Nelson Mandela*

At the time that Emma started at her new school, I took up a role with the justice department as a community visitor. This program came about as a result of a number of big, state-wide enquiries into abuse and neglect across mental health and disability.

The role was very challenging but I felt I was up for that. I believed that I would be able to make a difference in the lives of vulnerable people. I made regular visits to mental health units, and was responsible for visiting a number of group homes where people with disability lived. These homes were built after de-institutionalisation. I always found it interesting that staff in charge would say, "Oh yes, this is definitely their home". Then I would point out a number of very obvious things that indicated this wasn't a home. For example, there would be separate bathrooms for males and females, and no personal items such as photos anywhere in the house.

In one home I noted a line of tape across the floor at the kitchen entrance. I asked what this was for. "So they know not to come into my kitchen!" a staff member explained. But it's *their* home, right?! These were in no way homes; they were mini institutions. Some of the things going on in these group homes were appalling. I saw cases of financial abuse, sexual abuse and intimidation, and a complete lack of respect for people's dignity and rights. There was absolutely no understanding of how to help someone have a good life.

Also, just because you live in a house in a regular street doesn't mean you have a meaningful and relevant place within that community. If a person is living in a group home but has no contact with their neighbours or the wider community, they are still segregated and institutionalised. De-institutionalisation was meant to be a RE-MEMBERING, meaning that we are all meant to co-exist as members of one human community. "Difference" is not a fact; rather, it is the lens through which we choose to look.

There was very little community involvement at all. I recall visiting one site where all of the residents were profoundly disabled, with no speech or communication. The property was in a small street. I asked a staff member what the neighbours were like, and how the residents got along with them. She looked at me as though I had two heads and said, "We don't know the neighbours". Personally, I have always been keen to know who my neighbours are and to develop a relationship with them. A key part of a good life is relationships. A good life doesn't happen alone in your bedroom; it happens in relationship with others in your community. I suggested that the residents of this particular home might like to host some kind of get-together and invite the neighbours to join them. This suggestion was laughed at.

At one particular home I regularly saw staff take residents out shopping on a Friday afternoon. This is what I witnessed: the staff member loaded everyone into the van and, upon arrival at the shopping centre, loaded them out of the van. The staff member then walked into the centre with the residents trailing behind her like Brown's cows. No time, attention or thought was given to the state of dress or general appearance of the residents. The staff member would pull out a shopping list and push the trolley around the centre, picking up various items needed for the week. At no time were the residents engaged in anything to do with the shopping. On one occasion, I visited another site where, again, residents had been loaded into a van to "go shopping". One had breakfast down the front of his shirt, another wasn't wearing shoes, two did not have their teeth in and all of the residents looked untidy and dirty.

One day, I challenged a staff member about what I was seeing. The staff member then said, "Aren't you all about their rights? Don't they have a right to wear what they want?" I answered this by saying, "Yes, we all have a right to choose what we wear. But, we all have a right to be included and to be valued members of our community. The bigger part of your role, that you are paid to do, is to help these people be included in their community. How can that possibly happen when they are presented to the community looking like this?"

She had no reply. I then asked her, "If this was your mum that you were taking care of, would you want her to be out in public looking like that?" She said, "No. I always make sure Mum looks really good when she goes out". Sadly, it took some time for this staff member to realise what her role really was all about.

All of these residents had been institutionalised for most of their lives. They had no way of understanding how to move into and become a real and valued part of their community. That is what staff were supposed to be there for, to help the

"If this was your mum that you were taking care of, would you want her to be out in public looking like that?"

residents make the transition from institution to community.

Sadly, very often, I found that staff didn't seem to see the bigger picture, their real purpose for working with people with a disability. No doubt, for some, it was just a way to get an income.

I dearly wanted staff in these sites to understand the vitally important role they COULD play in the life of a person whose entire life had been determined by the routines and processes of an institution. I wanted them to help the people they were working with to discover so much – to discover who they were, now that they were no longer just another body in an institution. To help them explore for themselves what they liked to eat, drink, hear and feel. To uncover what made them happy and made them laugh, as well as what made them sad. To encourage them to find their voice and how to use it. To show them that this was THEIR life. To ask them, "How do you want to live your life now, and with whom?" I encouraged staff to see that their job was to set them free from the chains of institutionalisation.

I also tried to encourage staff to document the lives of the people they worked with (not just the usual details about their diagnosis or medical issues – it could mean engaging each person in the process by recording their voice or making a little video about them), so that a story might unfold for each wonderful, brave and precious person. I talked endlessly to staff members about how this kind of documentation might reveal all kinds of potential interests or hobbies for a person to become engaged in. If you could discover a hobby or interest that they had, it could be a bridge to taking their unique place in the local community. A story about a person's life would also be wonderful for their family to read.

Many times I used to wonder how the people in these homes could bear living the lives that had been assigned to them. How did they bear waking up to another day of meaninglessness, of hours to fill with nothing? Did they look out at the passing world and wonder about it or perhaps long to be part of it? Questions like these would often keep me awake late into the night.

Of course, I realised that encouraging people with disability to discover their value and interests was very difficult for most of the staff I spoke with – they had their masters to answer to. Also, most of the staff I spoke with believed they were doing a good job, and that the people in their charge had a good time. I recall a staff member in one site regularly telling me how much she loved her job of helping "these people". If only she had been helping.

At the end of each day I went home to my beautiful family, sometimes feeling paralysed by the horrors I had seen. I didn't know what kind of life lay ahead for Emma, but I was very clear about what would NOT be part of it – she would *never* live in a group home.

I have come to see that the only way we can steal from, abuse or neglect a person with a disability is if we have well and truly separated them from our reality. Separation destroys our ability to see our human brothers and sisters, and in our "not seeing" we trample their souls into the dust. We don't see their pain, suffering, hurts and sorrows as being as real as ours. We don't see that they will feel deeply the loss of a parent, just as we would. We don't see that the soul of a person with disability may long to find a creative outlet for their dreams. We don't see that isolation will be just as damaging to them as it is to any person.

We put criminals in prisons in order to isolate them from the community and to punish them. We take away their right to choose what to eat and who to eat it with. We restrict every aspect of their lives, right down to their privacy. But what crime have people with disability committed to warrant such cruel and inhumane treatment?

Earlier I mentioned that, when Emma was very young, she and I had visited a little group of people at a particular institution and introduced chanting to them. The institution had since closed down, and the young man with the angelic voice was living in a group home. I came across him in my role as community visitor. This beautiful soul was now lost in his own tormented world, and was unrecognisable. He was once again being described as being non-verbal, but now he had the added label of being "aggressive". There were restrictive practices in place. There was no one in this home who had been in the institution with him. However, there were a number of other residents with very challenging behaviours, and the level of aggression in this home was, at times, high. I am absolutely sure that if I were placed in a house where I had no choice about who I lived with and I felt under threat, I would be aggressive, too.

One day while I was visiting this home, the staff were occupied with the challenges of other residents. I asked where the young man was. I was told, "He's in his room. You can go and talk to him if you want, but he won't understand you". I knocked on his door and waited. I heard him sucking his hand, which I knew meant he was anxious. I approached and spoke his name. He made no response. I sat on the floor of his room and quietly began to chant the chant that, a few years earlier, he had chanted so sweetly. He didn't respond. I continued to softly chant, and after 20 minutes he got off the bed and sat beside me on the floor. He stopped rocking and began to softly chant with me.

In that moment, I felt overwhelmed with emotion and I had a sense of the struggle he felt in the house of torment that he had been placed in.

The next day, I did something that I was absolutely NOT supposed to do – I brought him a gift of a small CD player and gave him the chant on CD. Sometime after this, he had to go to hospital for a small procedure. He was understandably distressed, as anyone would be if they were not being told what was going on and where they were going. A staff member later confided to me that she took the CD and player to the hospital for him because she had seen the peaceful impact it had had on him.

It was truly a waste that such a beautiful voice was not being shared. I suggested to support staff and management that his voice could have led him to join any number of music-based community groups, and that this could well have been a bridge for him.

The pages of an entire book could be filled with stories of the appalling things I saw – on a regular basis – in these houses of horror.

I will finish this chapter with one last story. As I mentioned earlier, my role also included visiting mental health sites. One day, I was walking along an outside area and chatting to the residents, letting them know of the different ways I might be able to help them. One of the residents was sitting with his head in his hands. I approached him and said hello. He didn't respond. At that precise moment a staff member walked behind me and said, "No good talking to him. He's deaf. He can't hear you", and marched on.

I squatted down on the ground to make eye contact. I then signed, "Hello" and asked his name. He immediately looked up at me. He didn't sign back to me, so I tried again, this time spelling my name for him and asking what his name was. I think I will always remember the way he looked back at me. It was as though he was looking through a dense fog and couldn't quite be sure of what he was seeing. He signed back to me, "Your name". This confused me a little because I wasn't sure if he understood me or was just repeating me. So I waited for him. He began to cry and then signed his name. He explained that he had learned to sign before he had been brought to the centre as a young boy of 15 years of age. He then entered a world of total isolation, having no communication with another soul. At the time I met this gentleman he was 45 years of age. How does anyone live with that level of imprisonment? How is this called "care"?

It quickly became evident that he had a somewhat rusty but nevertheless good memory of sign. I spoke with the person in charge of the unit about getting support out to this man as quickly as possible. She was a very wise and compassionate woman, and she took steps immediately to get the signing support that this man so desperately needed. Having people with whom he could communicate opened a door for him, and he courageously took a step through into a world that had been denied to him for more than 30 years.

Abuse and neglect destroys our soul; this is the price we pay for separation.

A number of years after I had left the community visitor role, I learned that what I had been doing and talking to staff about was, in fact, Social Role Valorisation (SRV) – but more about that later...

CHAPTER 15

Look Beyond What You Think You See

"Each of us has meaning and we bring it to life."

— *Joseph Campbell*

hile I was confronting horrendous issues in my role with the justice department, Emma began to make it very clear that she didn't like school (despite now being in the state system, which was much more welcoming of students with a disability). I didn't ever feel that Emma didn't enjoy school because she wasn't bright; far from it. I also had no doubt that the first six months of her schooling had imprinted onto Emma the belief that "school is not a good place".

She was really quite clever, in her own way. Emma was also very skilled at getting out of a classroom when she didn't feel wanted. One year, Emma had a teacher who clearly didn't value the special needs students in his class. Whenever Emma was in his class, which was three times a week, she would make sure she was sent to the special ed unit within the first five minutes of class. The teacher asked me to come to the school to speak with him about Emma's behaviour. He explained that she would climb under her desk and refuse to come out and participate in any work, so he would send her to the special ed unit.

I asked him, "What do you think Emma's behaviour is trying to say?" He said he thought she just didn't want to do any of her daily work. I asked whether or not he thought Emma's behaviour might, in fact, be her way of communicating. He couldn't see that. So I pointed out the bloody obvious to him, which was that this behaviour only happened when Emma was in his class. I asked him whether or not he had noticed that it wasn't just Emma behaving this way in his class. I was aware that the three other special needs students in this class also made their way to the special ed unit every day that they were in his class. He was incensed. He said he thought that I was blaming him for how Emma behaved, and to this I said, "Absolutely!"

However, Emma was making it abundantly clear, every day, that she didn't want to go to school *at all*. No matter what I said to her about going to school, or how I said it, she always said "NO". I felt I was out of options because the school was now being very difficult about Emma's lack of engagement and increasingly difficult behaviour.

I found this time with Emma to be very challenging. I struggled to find ways to understand and help her. It felt as though she had retreated to some place where I couldn't reach her. At this point in my life there were times when I definitely had doubts about my ability to parent Emma. I was filled with fear and shame because sometimes I wondered whether or not I had made the right decision in bringing Emma home from hospital. There were times when I had no clue about what

*At this point in my life
there were times when
I definitely had doubts
about my ability to parent
Emma.*

her future might look like. Many times I felt like a complete fraud in my work as a community visitor, because my own daughter's life seemed to be spiralling downwards.

When I had reached probably my lowest point, I decided to step way out of the box and to seek answers from a very different perspective.

At the time, we had been going to a local homeopath to treat infections that Emma was experiencing. Emma seemed to like the homeopath who, as it turned out, used kinesiology as a tool to help determine which homeopathic remedy to use and at what dose. Emma had recently manifested a persistent rash right across her abdomen, so we headed off to the homeopath. He had previously told me that kinesiology was a useful tool in all manner of situations, so I decided to step off the branch and see where that might take us.

I asked him if he might be willing to work with Emma to see if he could uncover what was really going on within her. I wanted to know how she was feeling and how might I be able to help her. I had not told him anything about what was going on at school. The homeopath agreed to try, and to see what came up. It turned out that Emma was deeply unhappy at school and felt sad and frustrated at not being able to get her point across. She was confused about why she was in a place that made her unhappy. Her unhappiness was, in fact, the cause of the rash.

On another occasion I arrived to pick up Emma after school and was met by the head of the special ed unit and another staff member. Emma did as she always did and ran up to me, and I gave her a kiss and told her I loved her. She signed back, "I love you". At this point the two staff approached me and said, "We think this is the cause of Emma's poor behaviour". I was confused, so the head of the special ed unit said, "We think you should come and talk to us each first before you give Emma a hug or a kiss. You should first find out how she has behaved to see if she deserves a hug or a kiss". What a load of crap. Needless to say, I didn't bother with that heartless suggestion.

By now we were out of options for Emma because the school had decided they couldn't or wouldn't be able to help Emma. So the only place left was the special school.

The morning I took Emma to the special school (or as a friend of mine calls it, the not-so-special special school), I felt a deep and sickening sense of betrayal. I felt that the education system had betrayed us for forcing us down this road. But, mostly, I felt that I had betrayed Emma. After I dropped her off for her first day of special school, I had to pull the car over on my way to work because I was crying so hard. I was filled with a deep and sad regret. It was a real struggle to be going off to work each day advocating for the rights of people with a disability and mental illness while my own daughter was in a segregated school. Emma cut a very lonely figure at school, most of the time choosing to take herself away from everyone.

However, there were some bright moments during Emma's time in the not-so-special special school. In her first year there she became very fond of a boy in her class (I'll call him Barry). Barry had frequent seizures throughout the day. Right from her first day, Emma began to look out for him. At the end of each day she would get Barry's lunchbox from the fridge and put it in his bag. How did she know it was the right lunchbox and bag? Observation? Probably.

One day the school asked me to come to see the teacher. My first thought was, "Oh shit, what now?" The teacher and the aide told me that Emma was clearly fond of Barry. Not only was she fond of him, they also had some sort of special bond. They explained that they consistently observed Emma stopping what she was doing and going over to Barry. She would gently stroke him and say, "Okay, okay". The teacher told me this would take place just minutes before Barry had a seizure. Apparently Emma never got it wrong, and she always did the same thing, gently stroking him and saying, "Okay, okay". As the year progressed staff told me that they relied on Emma being the early warning system for Barry, particularly if they were out in the community for an event or outing.

Emma was clearly displaying ESP of some kind to be able to tap into Barry's energy in this way. Yet here she was in the special school, labelled as intellectually impaired. I often wondered if it was actually the education system itself that was impaired...

To try to counteract the negative feelings Emma had about school, I decided to enrol her in a dance school. She really enjoyed music, and often sang and danced at home. So I rang and enrolled Emma and noted down the class times. When I made the booking, I didn't mention that Emma had a disability; I simply mentioned that she enjoyed dancing.

We turned up for class on the first afternoon, and the instructor greeted us by hissing through her teeth, "Your daughter is disabled. You should have told me that on the phone". This was said in front of all of the other families waiting for the class to start. So I simply replied, "Well, I didn't realise that that would be a requirement for a little girl to simply enjoy the experience of dance. Besides, when I look around this room I see some children with blue eyes, some with brown eyes, and a couple with red hair. Did you require this information before accepting them?" My point is that you can find difference anywhere, if that is what you are looking for. The dancing school provided yet another example of the community's lack of empathy, compassion and kindness. Needless to say, Emma picked up on the feelings of the teacher and families and she didn't want to be there. She can also tell clearly when a person is saying one thing but is feeling something else, and at times this can make life quite difficult for her.

Teachers have the capacity to change a child's life in so many wonderful ways – conversely, they can also make their life difficult. Just two weeks into the first term of a new school year, I received a call advising me that the teacher wanted to see me. This teacher began by saying that Emma was being uncooperative and stroppy. Her next statement was an earth-shattering revelation about her lack of awareness. She said – and I am quoting her – "I am so surprised that Emma was placed in my class". I asked why that was. Her answer: "All the others in this class are quite intelligent". My response to her: "Well, in light of her uncooperativeness do you think she doesn't know how you feel? Perhaps, if you could change the way you see Emma she might change the way she responds to you". Surprise, surprise, nothing changed.

For that school year and the next it was very difficult to motivate Emma to get up and go to school. From what I could see, Emma really only enjoyed riding the bus to and from school and riding the adult tricycles around the schoolyard. Also, although Emma had been placed in a state-run special school, she was the only deaf child in attendance and had no one to sign to her (including teachers – there were no adults at the school who could sign). She must have felt so isolated and lonely, with no one to explain or share things. I raised this with the principal numerous times, but nothing happened. However, at the start of a fresh school year, a new principal was appointed and action was taken – she brought Deaf Services into the school, and this organisation's staff came with a great attitude of inclusion. They didn't just work with Emma; they formed a girls' signing group and a choir. I was very grateful to the principal for the genuine respect she showed Emma through her actions.

Within the first week of the new school year, I saw a shift in Emma. She started wanting to go to school. After about a month I happened to be at the school one day so I popped in to say hello to Emma and to meet her teacher. I was absolutely amazed that, in just a few weeks, this new teacher had a good understanding of what made each child tick. She knew exactly how to not only motivate Emma, but to inspire her to be her best self. In the two years that Emma had with this teacher, she learned more than during her entire time at school. Emma would have done anything for this teacher.

Why was this teacher successful with Emma when teachers before her were not? It's because she seemed to have a very genuine curiosity about each child and wanted each child to show her how they could learn. Emma made good progress in all areas, but particularly with communication. She stunned me one day when we were out in the car. When we stopped at the lights, she gave me a "weather report", saying, "Today is cloudy, Mum" (and it was). I was intrigued about Emma's willingness to show interest in something like the weather, but I was most interested to know how the teacher had fostered this interest. It turns out, it was pretty simple – she took the students outside to experience different kinds of weather. They also learned why the weather was relevant.

As part of this, the teacher had arranged for the students to do letterbox drops to a small number of houses around the school. This meant that the students were outside, so knowing what the weather was likely to be had relevance to what they were doing. A few years later I learned the hard way that if Emma could see how something might be relevant or useful, she was more motivated to learn more about it and apply it in her life. This concept could apply to any one of us.

I was very keen to get to know this amazing teacher a little better. We invited her to our home for dinner on a couple of occasions so she could see Emma in her own environment, and so that Emma could see her outside of the teacher role. Emma loved having her come to the house. What I found really interesting about this teacher was that this was her first time in a classroom of special needs students. She had a way of seeing the student, not their disability. I believe it was her way of seeing and being that most impacted Emma and the other students in the class. She saw possibility in each student and knew that it was her job to help them discover the power of that possibility.

Emma had a lovely teacher the following year, but she wasn't the same. However, by this time Emma was more receptive to learning and managed the year quite well.

At end of her final year of school, a graduation celebration was held for the year 12 students. Greg and I felt that Emma's finishing of school was an important milestone, just as it was for Roshan and Laksiri, and we loved having the opportunity to celebrate.

In the final weeks of school we had had a number of discussions with staff about what the future might hold for Emma. For the most part, staff seemed to feel that the only real option for Emma would be to place her in some kind of day facility. I didn't really know what Emma was going to do; however, I was very clear that it would not be at a day facility or anything like it. I knew she had to get a job and contribute to her community. But how would she do this? What work would she do? At that time, though, our family focus was on ensuring that Emma had a great night at her graduation.

One of Greg's hidden talents is sewing. Yep, he can sew really well, which is pretty good because I can't put a button on straight. He made Emma's dress, and she looked so beautiful in it and suddenly seemed so much more mature. Greg's mum came to join the celebration, as did my sister. It was a great night. Once Emma made it to the dance floor I didn't think we would be able to get her off it. I most loved seeing Emma dancing with her brothers; she looked so beautiful and full of fun and life.

Then, in the midst of all this joy, a sickening thought crept into my mind... What happens now? How do I take her life forward? How can she have a good life in the community? How? How? How? What am I going to do? As I sat watching her laughing and dancing, my smile concealed an inner fear that felt very urgent and powerful. The question, "What now?" felt like a rat gnawing at the very core of my being.

CHAPTER 16

The Search for Another Way

*"Be defined by a vision of the future, instead of
the memory of the past."*

— Dr Joe Dispenza

In the early days after Emma completed her schooling, it was very clear that she was lost, maybe even depressed. It was difficult to get her out of bed much before 9.30am and it wasn't hard to see why. What did she have to get up for? Although Emma had never really liked school, except for the two years that she had had with that very gifted teacher, it was now clear that school had at least provided somewhere to go each day, something to do – even if it was only to push back against it. Now, I was watching her sink into an abyss of nothingness. The faces of people in the group homes I had visited would haunt me as I watched her slip into an acceptance of boredom.

I knew that I had to do something to help her. I began by trying to get her to help with things like chores around the house and shopping. After an enormous amount of effort she would make savoury eggs one night a week. Trying to get her to leave her room to do this simple task was like pulling teeth. Each week she would drag herself begrudgingly out of her room to the kitchen, with her face looking as though she was being led to a torture chamber.

By 2014 Emma had been at home for two years, in her room. I had been looking online for ideas, for thoughts about how to take her life forward. I knew that she needed to be working in some capacity but I really didn't know how to help her achieve this. That year, discussion about Australia's National Disability Insurance Scheme (NDIS) was starting to gather momentum within the government and the wider community. I was a very enthusiastic supporter of the scheme, right from the time I first heard about it. I was hopeful that this scheme would offer a more level and fair means of providing support to all people with disability. I was very inspired that this scheme had come about as a result of the work being done on the United Nations' *Convention on the Rights of Persons with Disabilities*.

By this time we had some contact with a local disability provider. We organised for Emma to do some voluntary work for a local op shop, where she was encouraged to help with stacking things on shelves and vacuuming the floor. After several months of this, she refused to go anymore. I then looked into her doing some work with Meals on Wheels, also in a voluntary capacity. I was hoping that by getting her out of her room and meeting people, it might shift Emma out of her resigned mindset. I put a great deal of time and energy into trying to make this work for her. However, despite my best efforts, Emma once again made it clear that she didn't want to do this, either.

CHAPTER 17

Welcome Gifts

*"Have a mind that is open to everything,
and attached to nothing."*

— *Tilopa*

In around the middle of 2014 I invited my friend Karen and her husband David over for dinner. I spent a considerable amount of time talking to Emma before they arrived, letting her know that I would really like her to meet my friends. She reluctantly agreed to join us for dinner. She spent the entire time sitting right beside me, almost hiding behind me. She did manage a greeting, although without any eye contact. As soon as she had finished eating she went back to her room (her safe cave).

Karen and I had spoken before about the energy work that Karen did with people and some of the outcomes they had experienced. So I asked Karen if she would be willing to do some work with Emma. Neither of us knew how Emma would respond to this work, but I thought, "Well, we are all just energy, so this just might be the best way to communicate with Emma". It would be connecting with her at the soul level, where she does not have disability.

Karen and I spoke about what my vision was for Emma's life. I wanted Emma to become as independent as she could possibly be. I wanted her to know that her life was her own, and that she should be the one to determine the kind of life she wanted and who she wanted to live it with. I spent a great deal of time talking with Karen about my desire to get "out of the picture" so that Emma was not always looking to me as her guide. Emma was capable of so much more than she believed. I wanted her to know that when I am gone she could go on without me and still have a great life. I am not, nor should I be, her world.

Here is Karen's description of the energy work she does with Emma:

WORKING WITH EMMA

To connect and communicate with Emma, I use a combination of empathy and imagination. I imagine a safe place and then send a heartfelt invitation to Emma to meet me there. Everything is energy and thought is instantaneous, so our meeting place can be anywhere. It is up to Emma if she wants to meet with me, or not.

When Emma appears, I test her energy levels (physical, emotional, psychological, psychic and spiritual) to see where she is strong or weak. I work energetically to identify what issues may be going on for Emma and to bring those levels into balance. I then use empathy to connect with Emma to understand her point of view and to feel what she feels. In this way we can talk, without words. When I asked her what she wanted to be — what represented a grown and successful woman and the model for what is good and normal — Emma showed me her ideal, the characters from the television show Glee.

Once Emma's dreams were recognised, I used empathy to feel what held her back, what made her uncomfortable. Once those issues were clear, there was a way forward to coach and support Emma to overcome her fears and move towards her dreams. With practice, the connection became stronger, faster and clearer.

Karen Metcalfe

Karen's work with Emma was really quite miraculous. As a mum I have read many articles about the ways in which people on the autism spectrum might experience the world around them. But Karen was giving Emma a way of under-standing how the world around her worked and how she could get the best out of it.

CHAPTER 18

Seeking Answers

"We are limited, not by our abilities, but by our vision."

— *Abhishek Kumar*

For some time I felt that Emma having a business of her own would be a good way for her to move forward. My reasoning was that with Emma's communication challenges it was going to be difficult to find a "traditional job" for her. This was confirmed for me after I contacted an employment agency, asking them to help Emma find some kind of meaningful work. I was very flatly told that there was no possibility of finding work of any kind for my daughter. They suggested, "Why don't you look at putting her into a day centre so she can do some activities?" Most employment agencies look for the easiest way of filling spaces – if they have five spaces available, they want to find five people but not invest a lot of time and effort.

I began looking at businesses that were on the market; what was involved in keeping a business afloat; and how

I could create a role within a business for Emma. I looked at cafes, delivery businesses, newsagencies and a host of others – most were out of our price range. The frustrating thing about all of this was that I absolutely knew there was a way forward. I just couldn't see it – YET.

CHAPTER 19

The Real Experts

"In the universe there is an immeasurable, indescribable force which shamans call intent, and absolutely everything that exists in the entire cosmos is attached to intent by a connecting link."

— *Carlos Castaneda*

Over the years I have attended many presentations for families about "people with disability". These were presented mostly by "experts" who were talking about a syndrome or the characteristics associated with certain types of disability. I always felt as though I was being talked at, as though this person thought they knew all there was to know about the lives of people with disability. However, it seemed to me that they hadn't taken the time to get to know any of the people they spoke about. There was no thought of hope or possibility for a good life – just a never-ending lecture about what people might or might not be expected to do. To me, it often felt as though these kinds of presenters could have been talking about aliens. Sure, the subject of aliens is interesting, but unless you have actually lived with aliens then it's just theory. I once walked out of a presentation by an expert who had been brought to Townsville to speak to families about autism. There was no speaking *with* families, just talking *at* us. I walked out halfway through his "blah, blah, blah", and thought to myself, "Oh, shut up, dickhead; you don't know anything. Come back and talk to us when you have lived with autism 24/7".

I had been looking online for ideas about how I could help Emma become more independent and empowered. I had read many wonderful articles written by some pretty inspiring people, but I still didn't know which way to jump or how to start. I came across several articles about an organisation in Brisbane called Community Resource Unit (CRU). These articles featured stories of families who were definitely not following the herd. In other words, they weren't just doing the usual thing of placing their loved ones in a group home. These stories talked about individuals with a disability volunteering in their community, and in some cases they were living in their own homes. They were living lives that were more like those of other young people. The CRU examples were filled with great vision and hope for a good future. I really loved what I was reading and, in fact, I went back and read the articles several times. At the time I didn't realise that by reading and re-reading these articles I was starting the process of change within myself. I was beginning to see things differently.

Then something amazing happened. I received a flyer advertising an upcoming workshop with CRU, in Townsville. I decided to give it a go.

The workshop was not like anything I had seen or participated in before. It was powerful because there were real "experts" presenting – namely, people with disability and their families. The workshop had a profound impact on me because each one of the people with a disability had challenges with communication, just like Emma. But they took their place in front of the crowd and used a laptop or iPad to tell their stories. These were stories about lives that were being lived well, lives that had real substance. A support worker helped each person with the technology so that they could share how they lived independently in the community, and helped them to speak about the meaning-ful roles that they had. Their lives were embedded in the community, and their lives mattered. Each presenter, in their own unique way, laid out before me a map that we could follow to lead Emma to a good life of her own. This group of people was qualified to speak about disability because they lived with or alongside it every day.

My first thought was, "Wow, I can do this. First step: get Emma an iPad to help with her communication". The power of this workshop came not just from hearing disability being talked about. Rather, it was from people with disability telling their own story, in their own words. The technology – an iPad – was just a tool to support that. This workshop was focused on showing that people with disabilities can have self-determination.

It wasn't just the stories of the good lives that each person had been helped to craft that impacted me so strongly. It was seeing them in the role of "presenter" that was so challenging and moving. I had to admit to myself that I had never been brave enough to hold that kind of vision for Emma. This realisation hit me hard; it was a true "wake up". I understood that I had to get beyond talking and thinking about a "good life" and actually start helping Emma to create one for herself.

Throughout this workshop I could feel a shift happening within me that kept coming up in waves of emotion. It was like an oil rig shaking and shuddering as the oil is forcing its way up to the surface of the earth. The realities of what was needed was like the oil, forcing its way up through me to the surface.

As I drove home at the end of the two-day workshop I again felt a powerful surge of energy and emotion rise up within me. I had to pull over to the side of the road because I was sobbing so hard. Right there, in the car on my way home, I made an intention – a vow – that I would find a way for Emma to have purpose in her life. I was no longer fearful of the "how" question because I had made an intention to make a change. I knew that my intention would go out and bring back a way forward.

The next morning I decided to meditate on this unknown "how" so as to fuel it with even more power. I meditated with the intention of finding a way forward. I suddenly saw Emma sitting in the office at school where the year 12 students would sometimes do shredding and letter-folding. I initially thought I was losing my focus so I started meditating again, only to see Emma shredding, yet again. Then I realised, "This is it! This is what she will be able to do!" In that moment, I could see shredding as being a business for Emma. With stunning clarity and ease, a way came forward for Emma to have autonomy and control over her own life. Not only was I shown a way forward with a business; I could also see a whole new life for Emma. It was as though I was watching a movie about her life, only it hadn't yet happened. I was filled with gratitude for the sheer perfection of this vision.

For all of the time that Emma was at school I had tried so hard to help her to read (including engaging tutors) because I "knew" she would need to be able to do so to get some kind of job. But in this meditation I was shown a different kind of "knowing" about the way forward. The reading and writing just didn't happen for her. Now I could see that not being able to read or write was, in fact, the way forward for her. It would make her the perfect person to shred confidential documents. I later realised that if Emma went to individual businesses and shredded on site, the businesses would be assured of a double layer of confidentiality. Right now, as I am writing about the majestic, powerful experience of realising "the way forward" for Emma, I am again filled with emotion and gratitude. I know that the loving presence of something far greater than me was there once again, gently guiding me in the right direction – in the direction of purpose.

CHAPTER 20

The Way Forward

"Twenty years from now you will be more disappointed
by the things that you didn't do than by the ones you
did do. So throw off the bowlines. Sail away from
the safe harbour. Catch the trade winds in your sails.
Explore. Dream. Discover."

— H Jackson Brown, Jr

Emma had been receiving a disability pension from the government since the age of 17, and Greg and I had saved this for her. We now realised that we could use Emma's money to start her business. We began to investigate the world of shredders. Who knew there was so much to learn about shredders, from the different levels of security that various models offered (ranked by a DIN number), to where they were made, to whether or not they were cross-cut or straight? We initially bought a relatively small unit for Emma because she was just shredding at home for family and friends. It was clear that

Emma was happy shredding and got a lot of satisfaction from completing the task. I could see that it was something that somehow calmed her.

Greg and I began looking into registering the business for Emma – but first, the business needed a name. I had been playing around with some ideas, but each time I asked Em what she thought about a particular naming idea she would just say, "Oh, Mummy, no".

One day in the car, Greg and I were talking about a potential name for the business (Emma was in the back seat of the car). I knew that it would have to resonate with Emma so that she would be interested and engage with the name. Before we had gone out, Emma had been watching a Teenage Mutant Ninja Turtles DVD. Into my head popped the words "Master Shredder". I said, "Master Shredder – what do you think about that name, Emma?" She loved it and was laughing and signing, "Yes! Yes! That's the one". She then formed a sign like a Kung Fu pose and signed, "Me, Master Shredder". Having settled on a name, we set about registering the business in Emma's name and getting business cards printed. That was the easy part.

The obvious next step was to find a business that would give Emma an opportunity. I drafted a letter and sent it out to numerous businesses across the city. Sadly, the phone did not ring off the hook with offers of work. I knew I would have to look at this differently.

From that point on, I focused on businesses that used a lot of paper and had a need to destroy confidential documents. I sent a letter to a legal firm called Mackey Wales Law (the firm that had drafted our wills) to see if they might be willing to give Emma a go. I followed up with a phone call, which led to a meeting with one of the principals.

Emma felt uneasy about the idea of going into workplaces to do her shredding. She didn't understand why she should have to do this, because she was quite happy staying at home and shredding in the downstairs room. However, I pressed on, reasoning that Emma would see the benefits once she tried it out. When taking their first steps into the real world of work, most young people are awkward and fumble their way through.

Fortunately for us, the particular principal with whom we dealt in those early days was a very warm and gentle man. He approached Emma and her obvious unease with great respect. His lovely manner was no doubt borne of growing up with a brother who had Down syndrome. I had a strong sense that the principal knew better than most just what I was trying to do for Emma, and why.

I spent a lot of time attempting to show her the vision of the great life that could be hers... if she could just have a little courage. However, talking wasn't really getting us any-where. So I started to make picture boards of the vision I could see for her. This certainly helped. I found photos of Roshan and Laksiri in their work roles and placed them on a piece of cardboard, and Emma and I went to see the boys at work. I also found photos of Greg at work, and created an-other picture board with those. We spent time each day with the picture boards and talked about how her work would be helping people at the legal firm. We also did some role playing to show her how to greet people in the workplace. Emma understood the role-play concept, and in the safe cocoon of home she would happily play along.

Emma began paid work with Mackey Wales Law in January 2015, and soon took on other clients. This was a time of great change for her, because a new provider also came into Emma's life. Emma had become used to (and very fond of) a particular support person who did a few hours a week with her; however, as often happens in life, people move on to new positions. This opened the door for the lovely Rebekah to move into Emma's life. However, at first, Emma was very stroppy with Rebekah because she represented change. At the same time, Emma was trying to adjust to being out in workplaces, and they weren't all a natural fit for her. She was uncomfortable and unsure about the changes in her life, just as we can be about our own lives.

One of the ways that anger and frustration manifest in Emma is through her skin. These feelings show up as a rash or in the form of boils, often with several heads. This is very painful for Emma. At this time, she was particularly cranky and had several boils. So I reached out to Karen to see if she could help with the boils, and also to see if she could help Emma understand the vision for a wonderful life that I was holding for her.

After one of Karen's first sessions, a quite remarkable thing happened. Emma and I visited the speech pathologist who had helped set up different communication apps on Emma's iPad. This particular morning, Emma was very cooperative and took her work calendar to show the speechie what she had been doing since the last appointment. This was unusual behaviour for Emma; previously, she had been withdrawn and wouldn't engage. When the speech pathologist commented to Emma how proud she was of her and what she had achieved, Emma calmly signed, "I am a woman now".

I was so proud of Emma that when we got home I rang Karen to tell her how cooperative Emma had been. I mentioned that she had told the speechie that she was a woman now. Karen then shared with me that during Emma's session just a few days prior, they had been discussing the progress Emma had made with her work and that she was no longer a little girl but was now a woman. Emma had shared her desire to communicate better with people. This then led to looking at more ways to help Emma use her iPad to communicate her needs.

At the time that I was trying to get Emma's business off the ground, she did not receive enough funding to help our business-building efforts. Therefore, I took on the support-person role in those first tentative steps towards her future life. Each Tuesday morning before we went off to work at the legal firm, I made sure that we practised saying "hello" for her arrival and "thank you" for when she had finished her work. Just before we went through the firm's front door, I would quickly sign to her, "Remember to sign 'hello'". Emma did just that – without ever managing to make eye contact she would walk in, looking straight ahead, and sign "hello". I have nothing but admiration for the principals, partners and staff at the legal firm because they ALL – without exception – welcomed Emma. They made sure to sign "hello" to her each week and to thank her for her work, despite the fact that Emma never looked at them. They enthusiastically watched and listened to any news that Emma shared with them.

The principal insisted that Emma be paid for her shredding work. This provided a wonderful opportunity to discuss with Emma the concept of being paid in return for your work. At the end of her working day of two hours, we would come home and I would always talk to her about how well she had done that day. I would also encourage her to think about what she wanted to do with the money she had earned. Usually, we put it into the bank. However, sometimes, she would bust out and buy some new DVDs. I spent a lot of time instilling in Emma the importance of going to work, ensuring that she knew that she was making a difference and helping others, and that they appreciated it. She was also demonstrating to others that anything is possible, if you believe it is.

I told Emma that I was immensely proud of her, and that she was just like her brothers now, going to work. She became more comfortable with her work. My attention now turned to how to help her engage in some communication with people at the legal firm. For example, if we went to the

I told Emma that I was immensely proud of her, and that she was just like her brothers now, going to work.

movies on the weekend I would take photos and make a little story for her to take to work and share. I recall Emma making the choice to have her long hair cut into a bob, with some foils. Emma very much enjoyed showing off her new "do" through photos that showed her at the hairdresser – these gave her a way of sharing her excitement with others, just like any young person.

At around this time I was doing voluntary work for a crisis phone-line service. The organisation had a small, trouble-some shredder that worked only randomly. One day I spoke with the coordinator about Emma coming in and doing the shredding for them. The coordinator was very keen and supportive, so Emma began to work there one morning a week. Shortly afterwards the legal firm offered to speak to another legal firm about using Emma's services. So Emma then started at a second firm; they, in turn, opened the door for work with another firm. All of these legal firms have been so supportive of Emma and her quest for a good life.

Emma has a very special connection with the practice manager in one firm; I know Emma is fond of this lady be-cause she will always call from the firm to let me know if she didn't get to see her. I also see that the business man-ager cares deeply about Emma. She has bought Emma little gifts when she has gone on holidays. Each time she gives Emma a gift, my heart sings with sheer joy because I see how much Emma really values it. More importantly, I am so pleased that Emma has a way to give and a way to serve her community, and that she is valued for who she is, just as she is.

I felt that it was really important for Emma to communi-cate and connect with others at work. If I look at my own experiences of work, engagement with colleagues was often where I learned so much about the work I was doing and how to get better at it. Socialising with colleagues was just as important as the work. Those networks of colleagues and friends often remain in our lives long after we have left a role. All of these experiences build not only our skillset but our confidence in ourselves.

When any young person sets off to work for the first time, I see them as being a bit like a very young tree that has been removed from its cosy little pot and placed into a huge space of earth (I very much enjoy being in nature, and particularly love trees – so I think this is a great analogy). Initially, the young tree is a bit daunted and wilts a little. But, as it settles in, it sends down roots to hold and sustain it. Over time it sends out more roots in lots of directions to help it survive and thrive. With time and patience it can become a grand old master of the forest. This happens for young people when they first start out, with them putting down those initial roots, and feeling daunted. The new young worker then settles into the big wide world, with its myriad possibilities. Just as with the young tree's roots, they begin to widen their network of connections and friends in the workplace – connections that help them through the storms of their lives. The social connections and fun outings are a vital aspect of our work lives.

As I mentioned earlier, because of limited government funding, I was Emma's support person while she took those first shaky steps into her working life. However, to ensure that Emma could grow into her own unique and independent future self, I knew that this would have to be a short-term arrangement. Initially, when Emma was working I would sit close by so that she could see me. I would read a book – I got lots of reading done in those early days. Then I started to invent reasons to disappear. I would say, "I have to go to the bathroom" and then go down the back stairs and walk around the block a few times. At first, Emma would comment that I had been gone a long time. But, after a while, she began to be more focused on what she was doing and less focused on me.

During this time I started reading about business, and I began to see the uniqueness of the Master Shredder service. Although I didn't have formal training in marketing, I started to pay attention to what other businesses did to get their brand known. I learned that the keys to the success of any business is to determine its point of difference and to get the word out into the business community. I outlined Master Shredder's unique selling points, and joined a business networking group.

At the group's meetings, I shared the benefits for businesses if they engaged Master Shredder – firstly, the shredding is done on site, so no confidential documents leave the site until they have been shredded. Secondly, it offers a way for any business to embrace diversity. Thirdly, the service comes with a whole range of free gifts, such as:

- Emma's presence in the business lifting morale because people feel good about working for a business/organisation that is including her

- Emma inspiring other workers because they get to see what she has overcome to be there – they then realise that they can overcome challenges, too

- Emma demonstrating, just by her presence, that anything is possible – this speaks to the power of possibility

- The modelling of absolute honesty – Emma will always let you know what she thinks, straight up and with no sugar-coating

- The opportunity for workers to embody and practise tolerance

- Emma demonstrating that there is a purpose for every one of us to fill

- The modelling of a committed work ethic – Emma focuses only on work while she is working. She isn't checking Facebook or drinking coffee or smoking; she is just working.

- Emma bringing into every workplace the understanding that we are all students and teachers of each other

During the time I spent supporting Emma in her business, I couldn't count the number of times staff would approach me and tell me how proud they felt to be working for an organisation that was embracing someone like Emma. This often led to them telling me about a member of their family who had a disability, and that they hoped one day their family member might also be able to work.

My next step was to write to the head office of Queensland Country Credit Union (now known as Queensland Country Bank), of which we are members. In fact, I had opened my first account with them, and I still have it. My first letter seemed to fall on deaf ears. However, I am nothing if not determined. So I re-worked the letter and took it to a local branch manager. I spoke with her about what I was trying to do. She assured me that she understood and knew exactly who to send my letter to at head office.

At 8.30am one day, just as I was about to leave home for a meeting, I got a call from the HR manager at the credit union. He said that he had read my letter and that he was very moved by the passionate plea I had made on behalf of my daughter. He mentioned that he had spoken to the CEO and that they were both very keen to meet Emma and myself to talk about the possibility of Emma doing some work for them. I was so happy that I floated off to my meeting.

Later, I talked to Emma about the phone call from the credit union and said that they wanted her to help them. I obtained pictures of the credit union and, again, made a story for her. The reason I put so much time into creating stories was to help Emma see who she was becoming.

Sometimes I think that all of us need to take a breath and take in what we have actually achieved. It also gave Emma a way of understanding which workplace she would be going to, and who the people would be at that workplace. It showed her that she had a valuable place in the community. I was incredibly proud of her. She was getting great positive feedback from Greg, and Roshan and Laksiri were also very proud of her and often told her so. Each time Emma went to work, people told her how much they appreciated her. She was really starting to enjoy sharing her little iPad stories with people at her workplaces – their enthusiasm encouraged and motivated her.

I have so much admiration for the determination and courage Emma showed every time she walked into a workplace. It would be the equivalent of me suddenly finding myself in a work environment where nobody spoke English. I wouldn't be able to ask anyone for help or guidance, and I wouldn't have anyone with whom to simply chat. I am sure I would feel very isolated and perhaps even fearful. But Emma kept getting up and having a go.

On the day of the meeting with the HR manager and CEO of the credit union, I made sure that Emma had pictures and stories to share with them. Again, Emma was anxious about another new environment and new people. The meeting was an amazing experience. I expected that their focus would be on risk and how to manage it. However, I was very wrong. The question of risk never came up. In fact, for the entire hour, the HR manager and CEO were focused only on Emma and on how and what they would need to do to be able to support her. Their questions told me that they were committed to real inclusion.

I sensed that they felt they needed more understanding, and possibly support, from someone within the disability field, and that this would help them in their planning for bringing Emma on board. I suggested that my friend Ann, who was the head of a local disability organisation, speak with the HR manager and provide answers to their questions.

A week later, Emma started working at the credit union. The level of support for her was truly wonderful. Emails were sent out to the entire staff of 160-plus people, letting them know that Emma would be starting, and where she would be working and what her role was. At that time I was still her support person, so I saw firsthand the commitment the company made to having her there. Staff from all departments went out of their way to welcome Emma and me. While I had some concerns about still being in the support role, it gave me a great opportunity to get to know all of Emma's clients and to lay down good foundations. Every one of her clients feels like family, so if they need support we are there for them.

Emma was now working four mornings a week and she was settling into the rhythm of working for her four clients. However, the small shredder that we had originally bought for her just couldn't handle the workload and burned out. We replaced it a few times and then decided to do a bit of research into the costs and capabilities of a bigger commercial machine. We ultimately bought a $5000 shredder. Greg and Laksiri bolted it to a strong commercial trolley to make it easier to move it around. The new machine could certainly do a lot more work and at a quicker pace. However, it weighed 100kg, so now we had to get a car that could transport it. We originally bought a utility and added a metal cupboard to the back to house the shredder. We also installed a lift on the side of the tray to lift and lower the shredder. But in 2015 we purchased a second-hand van that was designed for a wheelchair – it had a built-in hydraulic ramp, which made loading and unloading much easier. In 2016 we purchased a second commercial shredder with a bigger motor, which meant it had the capacity to work all

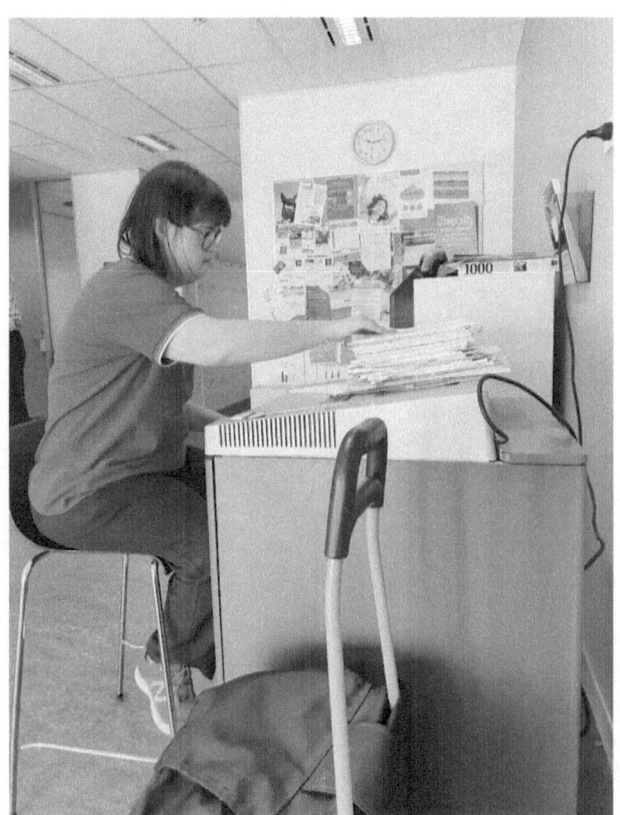

The Master Shredder, hard at work

day. The second shredder is a backup when the primary shredder is down for servicing.

I am incredibly proud that all of the equipment bought for Emma's business – including the vehicle – was paid for by her. Greg and I researched the purchases, but it was Emma's money that paid for everything. The business and the car are registered in her name.

Emma's business cards feature one short sentence that sums up her story:

MASTER SHREDDER: POWERED BY POSSIBILITY, NOT DEFINED BY DISABILITY

CHAPTER 21

Gathering Allies

*"As you grow older, you will discover that you have
two hands, one for helping yourself, the other
for helping others."*

— *Audrey Hepburn*

In 2015 our service provider took on a new state director, a truly inspiring lady called Lorna Sullivan. Lorna spent time talking with me and other local families about support circles. She spoke of her experiences with support circles in New Zealand and of how invaluable it could be to have a group of committed people around a family. Support circles are not paid or formal structures. They are a creative network of interested people who are invited to come together around a person with a disability, and their family, to offer friendship and support. Members of a support circle are not responsible for "caring" for the person; the hope is that, if asked, they will give their time to "look out" for the person.

Initially, I was daunted by the prospect of inviting people to join us on this journey of discovery with Emma. To my astonishment, no one we asked said, "No". They were all honoured to be asked, and each member brought their own gifts, insights and understandings to the group. As Emma's mum, sometimes it can be a very real struggle to see past my own fears and concerns and to view things from a different perspective. However, the support circle members didn't have the emotional attachments and the fears that I sometimes had, so they were able to help me go forward into new territory.

Our first couple of gatherings were a bit clunky, but as we all got to know each other the circle began to function quite well. In the beginning, the focus was on trying to secure more work for Emma. Two of the support circle members proved to be very helpful in this regard, because they quietly worked on opening the door for Emma at a large government department. It took almost a year for the department to take on Emma, but it has proven to be a wonderful, supportive place for her to work. She is valued and respected there, not only for her work, but for who she is. I wondered how she would cope in such a big workplace, and it certainly took her a bit of time to find her feet. But I can only express my gratitude to the people in charge of the department for their genuine support, and for their concern for Emma's wellbeing. They embraced Deaf Services coming to the workplace to provide staff with insight into deaf culture and to teach some signs.

It is a very humbling and uplifting experience to be surrounded by people who have made the choice to give you the gift of their time and energy. I was always in awe of our support circle, this group of people who kept coming back to meetings with open minds and willing hearts. They just wanted to help realise the dream of Emma having a good life, a life that at its core is rich in experiences, a life that is hers to live as she chooses, a life that looks like everyone else's – an ordinary life.

Woven into the cloth of the ordinary shines luminous the strand of the extraordinary...

CHAPTER 22

KISSing Housework

"The greatest achievement was at first and for a time a dream. The oak sleeps in the acorn; the bird sleeps in the egg; and in the highest vision of the soul, a waking angel stirs. Dreams are the seedlings of realities."

— James Allen

We have a highset home with a downstairs living area built in. When Emma was 21 years of age I spoke with her about moving into a room downstairs. We added a kitchen and Emma made the move. We also installed a door at the bottom of the stairs to show Emma that there was a distinction between what was now her space and what was ours. I would always knock before I went into her space, and without saying anything Emma would, in turn, knock on the door before coming upstairs. For me, it was very important that she begin to see the downstairs area as her space, her home, because I intended to introduce the idea of her moving out altogether at some point in the future. But first I wanted her to understand the concept of a space to call your own and the responsibilities that come with that.

Emma was keen to move downstairs because the thought of having all that space to herself was very appealing. She was also thrilled to have a bigger TV. However, I did explain that there were some rules that went with the move. She had to keep the area clean and tidy, and she would now be responsible for doing her own laundry and cooking.

All of a sudden Emma was much more enthusiastic about cooking and cleaning. I learned a very valuable lesson – when activities have a relevance to her life, Emma is quick to get involved. As I mentioned in an earlier chapter, when Emma was at school a teacher made noticing the weather relevant to what the class was doing. Although I had previously tried to teach her to cook, and to encourage her to clean her room, I could now see that this made no sense to her. In her mind, it was my house so why should she clean it or cook in it? However, it made perfect sense that she would cook in her own space. In fact, it didn't take her long to learn how to cook quite a few dishes.

I overcame potential safety issues with the stove by employing the KISS method (Keep It Simple, Sweetheart) – I bought five bottles of fingernail polish of different colours and painted a colour next to each hotplate. I then painted the same colour next to the corresponding switch. This meant that Emma would know which hotplate was on. Simple. Emma picked up the concept right away. I also laminated pictures of ingredients and put them up on the kitchen wall. When she had learned how to prepare a dish without any support, I would take a photo of the dish and put it up on the wall. This provided her with a way of choosing what she wanted to cook each evening. None of the dishes I was teaching her to cook were complex, but they were healthy and relatively simple for her to achieve.

Teaching Emma to cook required some out-of-the-box thinking. Emma learns a great deal just by watching, so I provided demonstrations and repeated them for her. I recall the night she decided that she would cook spaghetti for the first time. The simplest way for Emma to know how much water to put into the saucepan was to show her that she needed to use two of her big blue cups. However, when it came time to empty out the boiling water and drain the pasta, Greg was terrified that she would burn herself. He couldn't watch, so he would go back upstairs. However, I knew Emma would follow my lead. So I reassured her by saying, "If Mum can do it, so can you. Just watch what I do, and then you do it". She copied what I had done and tipped out the water into the sink, all without any drama. She then moved on to the next task.

Understanding how long it takes to cook pasta is a bit difficult, so I purchased a timer and put a sticker on the 10-minute mark. We added pictures to her wall that showed her what was needed to cook spaghetti. Emma had, and still has, several timers that are each used for cooking different things. For example, there is a timer with a sticker for the time it takes to cook fish, a timer for pasta, and a timer for cooking chips in the oven. Emma now has a slow cooker, which makes life a whole lot easier for her because she can "set and forget" the cooking of her evening meal.

I also used stickers with the washing machine to indicate the buttons that she needed to use. The first day on which I heard Emma get up and put on her washing without any help was so gratifying. She was starting to become more capable with her life downstairs, and took great pride in showing me that she had done something like folding her washing without being prompted. (If you'd like to see how we've set up Emma's kitchen and laundry to help her be independent, head to her page on my website: joannelynam.com/emma.)

However, we did have a few challenges when it came to Emma cleaning the downstairs room. I think it's fair to say that she has inherited her mother's lack of enthusiasm for cleaning. But I did make it clear that cleaning was all part of the deal. I often had to reiterate to her that the arrangement was to keep it clean or move out. She understood.

Emma really loved her space and was always very keen to show it off to visitors. She spent about 18 months living downstairs. During this time we held regular monthly support circle meetings in her space. We could have had the meetings upstairs or out at a café or restaurant but I felt there were a few good reasons for having the meetings in her space. Firstly, it provided a social opportunity for Emma. Secondly, it gave her the opportunity to be the host for the meetings. This meant she was responsible for welcoming her guests and inviting them into her home. I can't begin to describe how immensely proud I felt the first time Emma got up and welcomed each circle member into her home. It also gave Emma the chance to show off her cooking skills – she would usually choose to make pizza for everyone. Being the person in the position of providing service is so often denied to people with disability. We all need to be able to give and receive to have balance in our lives.

Thanks to the help of Lorna Sullivan, Emma was able to receive more funding. This meant we could start to employ more support people, and I could help Emma see the bright future that was just ahead, waiting for her beyond me. As I mentioned earlier, Lorna was the new director of the provider we were with at the time. Lorna was taking this provider into a brave new world, which I, for one, just loved. Whenever Lorna came to Townsville it was always great to spend time with her; I would come away feeling that my vision had grown, and that I had gained a little more understanding of how to continue to help Emma grow. Lorna often commented on the huge growth and changes that

Emma really loved her space and was always very keen to show it off to visitors.

she would see in Emma each time she visited. This is really helpful for a parent to hear, because it's hard to admire the view when you are up to your armpits in alligators.

While Emma was living downstairs I introduced her to the idea of having a holiday without Mum and Dad. When we researched things that were of interest to her, we suggested she might like to go to the Gold Coast to see some of the theme parks. I showed her the theme park websites so that she had some idea about what she could do and see. At the time, Rebekah was her support person – Emma really liked her, and Rebekah was delighted to be taking Emma on her first holiday. Because this was a big step, we planned for Emma to be away for a few days only, just to give her a taste of what a big life of her own might be like. She really enjoyed visiting the theme parks and staying in a lovely hotel. Having fun was the primary goal for this trip, and Emma certainly enjoyed herself. It was also clear that she fretted a bit, which was evident by the number of times she rang me. But the seed of her future life was planted and it started to grow. Even though this was only a small trip, it showed Emma that she was fine without Mum. This was a huge boost to her confidence, just as it is for any young person the first time they take a holiday without Mum and Dad.

Anyone who knows me will tell you that I am no IT geek. As another way for me to step away, I handed the iPad and story-writing over to Rebekah. Delegating this role allowed me to focus on what I was good at – the vision. The speechie was really helpful in recommending different apps to consider for Emma's communication. One of these was called Pictello, and it has been one of the best purchases we have ever made for Emma. Pictello is a story-telling app – you upload photos or pictures and add text to accompany them. Once set up properly, the app will then verbalise the text. Emma began using this at support circle meetings to share news about her workplaces, a new client, or a trip to the movies. It also allowed her to share with people at work what she had been doing outside of work. As I mentioned earlier, social chit-chat at work is an important strand in the fabric of any good supportive workplace. No doubt, if Emma was left to her own devices she would just go in, get the shredding done and leave – there would be no growth opportunity for her or for others. Chit-chatting about her life did a couple of things. It gave her confidence to further engage (because it showed her that she was not just accepted – she was welcomed) and it gave people in the workplace a glimpse into who is the person behind the mask of disability.

One day Rebekah suggested that Emma might like to try a Zumba class because it had great music and movement. Emma really enjoyed Zumba, and ended up going by herself to another class during the week. When I first mentioned this extra Zumba class to Emma she was very keen, even after I explained that Rebekah wouldn't be able to go with her. I was blown away when she still wanted to go completely on her own. The first afternoon I dropped her off at the class with her phone, asking her to call me when she had finished. She got out of the car and confidently walked into the class, handed over her money and joined in.

Emma didn't know that I was, in fact, watching from a distance. What I saw for quite a while was that the other ladies seemed very uncomfortable about having a young woman with a disability in the class. But over time the class came to be a wonderful supportive environment for Emma to explore her independence and to discover how she would like to communicate in the class, and with whom. Again, the iPad was a very useful tool for this. Her decision to attend the extra class spoke volumes about just how far she had come in her life. She had gone from being a withdrawn young woman who didn't want to leave her bedroom to a strong, determined young woman who loved Zumba.

Living downstairs provided Emma with another opportunity for her to step forward in life – she could learn to do her own shopping. I wanted her to understand that food and other necessities don't just appear in your cupboards, which is what had happened for her up until that point. If she was to be truly independent, she needed to learn how to shop for those things herself.

I approached shopping using the same KISS concept that I used for cooking. Because Emma couldn't read, I took photos of the items that she needed to buy. I then laminated them and put them on a key ring. The aim was that Emma would eventually take a taxi on her own to the shops and to do her shopping by herself. I asked Rebekah to work on this with Emma because they had been working well together for a little while. Emma was clearly very fond of Rebekah and trusted her, as did I. I also knew that Rebekah understood the importance of Emma learning how to shop for herself and that the end goal was for her to have a greater level of independence.

So that Emma could get used to travelling in taxis, to begin with Emma and Rebekah went in a taxi together. Before their first outing to the shops, I went to the supermarket with a photo of Emma and my contact details. I explained to the manager that Emma would come with Rebekah initially, but that Rebekah was not there to assist with the shopping. She was there to help Emma learn how to help herself. For example, if Emma couldn't find or reach an item, Rebekah was not to help her. Emma had to go to the front counter with her iPad and use it to ask for help (by showing the staff what she needed). When she had finished shopping she would also use her iPad to ask staff to call a taxi.

It didn't take Emma long to learn where things were and, if she found herself stuck, who to ask. The next step was for Rebekah to get herself out of the way. I suggested a similar strategy to the one I had used when working with Emma in her shredding business – just making an excuse to leave. After a little while, Emma quite liked shopping by herself and began to ask Rebekah to wait outside the supermarket. Rebekah was very respectful and would hang back outside. Of course, she was still nearby, if needed. Eventually, Emma made it clear that she wanted to go completely on her own. One day she made this point after shopping by getting into the taxi without Rebekah (who had been waiting outside and was distracted by a request for help by an elderly lady) and coming home by herself. I talked to Emma about why she had done that, and she was very clear that she felt she could go shopping on her own.

However, Rebekah and I were a bit sneaky. After that first unsupervised trip home, Rebekah would go to the shopping centre ahead of Emma and hide. She would then text me when Emma had finished shopping and was in the taxi. There were a couple of occasions when there were misunderstandings on the part of the taxi driver, and Rebekah was able to step in and resolve the issue. After that we made some laminated cards featuring directions, and Emma was able to give those to the driver.

Rebekah was very conscious of the shopping goal: Emma was to be as independent as possible. Eventually, Rebekah found another app that would allow Emma to upload pictures of grocery items directly to her iPad; this eliminated the need for laminated cards. As well as leaving Emma to shop on her own, Rebekah downloaded the taxi app onto Emma's phone and showed her how to order a taxi. It was just a matter of repeating the steps for Emma until she could manage it for herself. I would pinch myself each week when Emma would arrange her taxi and go off to do her shopping independently. Being able to do "ordinary" things like these was only possible because I had a strong vision for Emma – I wanted her to have the same rights and freedoms as everyone else. Support staff were also crucial because they understood the vision and the role they played in bringing it to life, and technology also played a huge part. These factors all helped Emma to achieve a great level of independence.

CHAPTER 23

Looking Through an SRV Lens

"Justice will not be served until those who are unaffected are as outraged as those who are."

— Unknown

O ne day a local disability provider asked how I came up with the concept of the Master Shredder business. He had lots of questions about how businesses had responded to Emma working with them. He asked if I had had any exposure to disability before starting the business for Emma. So I started telling him about my time with the justice department and of the sad, pathetic existences lived by most of the people I visited. I shared the discussions I so often had with staff about how they could choose to help set their clients free from the chains of institutionalisation or, conversely, perpetuate their client's institutionalisation.

They could continue to be prison wardens or could become lightbearers – the choice was theirs.

The disability provider said, "You're talking about SRV – Social Role Valorisation". He explained that a doctor called Wolf Wolfensberger had come up with this concept back in the 1970s. He mentioned that there was an SRV workshop coming to Townsville. I decided to attend, and I absolutely loved it. The concepts shared felt about as familiar and natural to me as my own arm. I knew exactly what the instructor was talking about and why it mattered. I had somehow intuitively known this when I was working with the department. It turns out that the things I had been saying and suggesting to staff in group homes, all those years back, could have been lifted straight out of an SRV manual.

I am not a qualified SRV teacher, so it is not my intention to provide an in-depth understanding of SRV here; rather, I want to show how I have used it to underpin the vision for Emma's life (for that matter, it can also be applied to so many areas of our regular community life). While the name "Social Role Valorisation" is a bit of a mouthful and could seem intimidating, if you are a parent of a child with a disability I strongly urge you to look past the name and to explore the concept. Please take a leap of faith and look for an SRV group or teacher – there is a lot of information online, including listings of local teachers. For me, the steady, grounded principles of SRV are like a compass, providing a reference point for those times when I feel a little lost. With our busy lives, in which we sometimes feel as though we are in a washing machine, it's great to have help to stay on track.

SRV questions why some groups of people are devalued in our society, and investigates what can be done to change their devalued status. Examples of devalued groups include the elderly, people who have a mental illness, people with a disability, indigenous people, refugees, asylum seekers and people who don't speak a local language. What

SRV questions why some groups of people are devalued in our society, and investigates what can be done to change their devalued status.

Wolfensberger came to understand was that our different career roles afford us greater or lesser status in relation to other people. For example, a judge or barrister is afforded more value and status than a cleaner. Wolfensberger eventually discovered that if you can provide a devalued person with a visible and valuable role, you change their devalued status to that of valued. The focus of SRV is on roles, not activities. It also considers a person's image and what would be considered typical for a person of the same age. For example, it would not be typical for a 90-year-old woman to want to start listening to heavy metal music, but it is more likely for a young person in their 20s to do so. SRV also discusses the wounds that have been inflicted by society's rejection.

Steven Hawking is a good example of a person with a disability having a valuable role. Within the scientific community he is respected for his contribution to science, so his role as a scientist afforded him value – despite his quite significant disability.

At the time of writing, in Australia we are seeing a couple of very good examples of people being devalued. The devaluing comes from a lack of community discussion and media coverage. There is currently underway a royal commission into violence, abuse, neglect and exploitation of people with disability, as well as a royal commission into aged care quality and safety. Prior to these there was a royal commission into misconduct in the banking, superannuation and financial services industry.

The latter drew huge interest and media coverage, with daily insights and outcomes from the commission appearing on our screens throughout the day. It was the subject on everyone's lips. One could hear snippets of conversation about it in shops and restaurants and all over social media. However, the same level of interest, discussion and news coverage has not been the case for the commission into aged care – the coverage of this commission dropped to the occasional news story. The media coverage for the commission into disability was limited to its opening and we have seen very little coverage since.

What does all of this tell us? From the perspective of SRV, the elderly and people with disability are not seen as valuable. However, banks, which make profits, are seen as valuable, even though many have been shown to be guilty of multiple wrongdoings.

So, what are the qualities of the "valued ones" in society? Firstly, we value youth – our western culture worships this. Secondly, we place great value on physical fitness and sporting prowess – millions of dollars goes to promoting and engaging in sport, and we label the young participants with the mantle of "hero". Thirdly, we are obsessed with a very narrow ideal of beauty – it only comes in one size... small. Fourthly, at all levels of our culture we value production – producing more profit at work or a gold medal or win for your team. The fifth quality is money – the more of it you have, the more valuable you appear to be.

There are a few keys things to keep in mind around SRV. Here are the concepts that I feel are really important:

ROLES, BUSYNESS & MEANING

Being busy is not the same as having a valued role. As a culture, we are very focused on being busy. In Townsville I see a lot of people with disability being transported to facilities where they are effectively warehoused all day. It is there that they are kept busy doing meaningless activities.

Busyness is like a magic show that distracts you, making you look "over there" while the magician does something else. While people with disability are kept busy with mindless activities, they don't notice that they don't currently have meaning in their lives. Also, it makes mainstream society feel better about people with disability and what to do with them – keep them busy and out of the way. This is apparently acceptable. But would people without disability feel satisfied and happy at being kept busy all day, for the sake of busyness?

VISIBILITY

My vision for Emma rejected the damaging notion of "busyness". I wanted her to be in a work role where she was visible, where she was valued and where she contributed in a way that she would enjoy. In her daily role as the Master Shredder, she is a very visible presence in the businesses where she works. This is important. If she was locked away shredding in some unknown and unnamed warehouse, it would be giving in to the expectation that history has allotted to people like Emma – to be invisible. When organising clients for Emma, I paid a great deal of attention not only to the business itself but to where she physically works within each business. I have gone to great lengths to ensure that she is known at the different levels of each business. To this end, I have made presentations to different businesses and government departments to ensure that she is known and valued. I also secured some funding to enable Deaf Services to go in to some of Emma's original clients (you may remember me mentioning this in chapter 21) to provide training for staff around sign language and its culture. This would help Emma to be valued for who she is, as she is.

Emma's business allows her to be visible in the wider community, too. The business can generate a lot of shredded paper, and the bulk of it goes to a local avocado farm where it is used as mulch to help with water conservation and weed control. A small portion of the shredded paper is used by our family to create handmade paper, as well as paper products such as greeting cards, writing sets, art books and decorative paper bowls, and bricks for use in a barbecue. These are then sold at a local night market. This gives Emma another very visible role – that of a stallholder. The markets also provide Emma with an opportunity to engage with different people. She is able to use her iPad to tell passing shoppers about her business.

Ever since she was quite young, Emma has had a keen interest in live theatre. I thought it might be good to get her actively involved with a local theatre company. So, for several years now, she has worked as a front-of-house volunteer for a theatre company. This gives Emma a very fun visible role. Although she has very little spoken language, she is able to use her iPad to help sell programs (she sets up the Proloqu2go app to ask the question, "Would you like to buy a program?") and she enjoys getting to watch the show. I am very proud of Emma and what she is achieving. Seeing her take the opportunity to step into a very visible role says a great deal about how much she has grown.

THE "TYPICAL"

What's typical? This question continues to form a huge part of the planning and forward thinking around Emma's life. It involves looking at her life and asking, "What do other young people her age do with their lives?" It's the everyday things that young people do – they go to work or study of some kind, and they spend their leisure time going to movies, theatres, restaurants and clubs. Young people move out of the family home, and as they get beyond the family gate they begin to discover themselves outside of the roles of sister, brother, son or daughter. They try new things and experience the world from a fresh perspective. They make new friends, they travel and they go to concerts to see their favourite bands play. They take on the identity of "living on my own" (or with mates), and this brings the necessity of learning new skills such as cooking and cleaning, and the chore that is laundry. These experiences open them up to an entirely new world.

When Roshan and Laksiri moved out, initially they each rang to ask for recipes and instructions. However, over time they dropped the recipes I had given them and discovered their own ways of doing things. Both are now great cooks with very different tastes in food. They also learned the hard way that if you don't do your laundry, you end up with nothing to wear.

When young people move out on their own they grow into their unique magnificent selves. A tiny seed holds the vision and holds all that is needed for it to become a grand old lady of the forest. The majesty to create and become whoever they want to be lies within ALL young people, if they are given the opportunity to realise it. My vision for Emma was – and still is – that she live in a way that is typical for any young woman of her age. This means that she is free to make decisions about her own life and isn't segregated from the rest of society.

IMAGE

This refers to how things "look", and it is really important. If you cast your mind back to my experiences with disability group homes in the community, you will recall that I spoke about people going to the shopping centre in dirty clothes and without shoes. Being dressed this way made it much less likely that anyone would be willing to engage with them. This image says that this group of people clearly have a disability, they can't take care of themselves, and they are not capable. With the support worker holding the shopping list and putting what was needed into the trolley, other shoppers are silently told that this group of people isn't even able to do their shopping. It portrays them as the perpetual child, as helpless, useless. On the other hand, if the residents had all been well dressed and each given pictures or a list of items to put into the trolley, it would have shown them as being much more capable and competent.

When Emma started working, one of the first things we did was to get a work uniform for her. When support staff began working with her, it was important for the staff member to be seen in the same uniform. This was so that when they walk down the street towards a business, anyone watching would just see two people who work for a business called Master Shredder. To a person passing by and noticing Emma, the message is one of competence, ability and usefulness. Just like many other businesses, Emma's car has signs on the rear and sides – to anyone driving past it looks as though the car is advertising just another shredding business. Whenever Emma is out in any setting she is always well dressed. While I know she would love to wear a *Lion King* T-shirt, I am mindful that if she was to wear this out in public it would immediately cast her into the role of "little girl". On the other hand, when she goes out wearing her *Rocky Horror* T-shirt, it shows her as a normal, funky young woman.

If food is hard in texture, Emma has difficulty cutting it up to eat. I ensure that staff know that if they are out for a meal or snack with Emma, it's REALLY IMPORTANT to ask that her food be cut up in the kitchen and brought out to her that way. To have staff cut up Emma's food in public would send a poor message about her, implying that she is not capable of feeding herself, that she is a child. I have seen many examples of a well-meaning support person cutting up a person's meal in a restaurant with other diners watching on. Again, the message is: "Oh, the poor person with a disability isn't capable".

I once had a support person show me a video she had taken of Emma at the zoo. Emma likes lions and tigers, and in the video she was standing at the lion enclosure growling like a lion and signing the word for "lion". When I spoke to the support person I asked her to look at the video and consider what the people watching Emma might feel about seeing her growl like a lion. Of course, they would see her as a child, which she is not. She was, at that time, a 24-year-old woman. As part of staff training, I explain that there may be times when Emma behaves in a childlike way. I ask them not to engage in this behaviour, and instead to remind Emma that she is a woman and not a child. It's about bringing Emma up to the level of identity associated with people who don't have disability.

My other pet hate, which I have mentioned previously, is when support staff wander aimlessly around a shopping centre with a person with a disability. It's fine to go to a shopping centre, as long as there is a purpose for being there – not just to fill in time. If the trip to the shopping centre is to meet someone for a coffee, or to look for a new outfit, shoes or DVDs, then there is a purpose for being there. Everyone working across the disability sector has a responsibility to ensure that the people they are working with are seen as mature, and are seen in a positive light. Mindlessly wandering around a shopping centre sends a subtle but powerful and disempowering message that people with disability only need to be entertained or kept busy, and that this is all that can be expected of them.

Recently, I saw another example of this kind of mindless action. I watched a support person completely devalue the young woman she was working with, in a very public setting. She brought the young woman, who was in a wheelchair, into the shopping centre. About halfway down one of the aisles, the support person saw a pop-up stall selling clothing. The support person stopped abruptly, right in the middle of the aisle. She then left the young woman sitting there so that people had to move around her. The support person took her time looking at different articles of clothing, and finally purchased one. At no point did she even ask the young woman – whom she was being paid to support – if she minded being left in the aisle. She could have turned the wheelchair around and had the young woman look at different articles of clothing and feel the different fabrics, and even ask her opinion about styles and colours. No, she just left her in the aisle. This sent a very clear message to every person in the shopping centre – the young woman in the chair wasn't worthy or capable of being engaged in the simple act of looking at clothing.

When Emma goes to do her weekly grocery shopping at a local shopping centre, it's important that she is well dressed and that she knows how to ask for help if she needs it. I recall that when Emma first started to do her own shopping, Rebekah would be in the background taking photos. One day Rebekah showed me a photo she had taken of Emma at the checkout – in the photo you could clearly see a number of shoppers watching Emma with great surprise. A young woman with Down syndrome doing her shopping on her own was not something they had seen before. It quietly challenged what they believed was possible. It also demonstrated that the role of independent and capable shopper is not one that they associate with a person with a disability.

Whenever Emma is out for morning or afternoon tea, she is responsible for placing her order and paying for it. It is not OK for support staff to take Emma's card and order and pay on her behalf. Emma is capable of using her iPad to place and pay for her own order. I always tell staff that if they do things for Emma that she is capable of doing, they are effectively stealing from her. They are stealing her independence, and they are portraying Emma as a child who needs help.

The concept of image can apply to aged care, too. I regularly see paid support staff out with an older person and making a good job of devaluing them. How do they devalue them? Firstly, by wearing a uniform and ID tag that

A young woman with Down syndrome doing her shopping on her own was not something they had seen before.

identifies the provider they work for. This lets everyone know that this older person doesn't have any family or friends to take them shopping. It says that they aren't valued or capable of much, and that they are like children who must be accompanied to the shopping centre. Secondly, it is demeaning for paid staff to take the older person's card and order and pay for their coffee. It portrays the person as not being competent enough to pay for a coffee, again reinforcing the image that they are like a child who has to have everything done for them.

A WIDER APPLICATION

Here is one final way in which you can use the lens of SRV to see the world. In shopping centres all over Australia there are parking spaces for parents who have toddlers and infants. Logically, you would think that the community group that would most benefit from parking closer to the shops would be older Australians. The group with infants and children are clearly fit and healthy, and very much able to walk a little further to the shops. So why do the young and fit parents get the preferred parking? I believe it's because they are more likely to come to the shopping centre frequently and therefore spend more money – this makes them a more valuable group in the eyes of the shopping centre. We see this again with entertainment being provided for children during the school holidays. Why isn't this available for lonely older Australians? Because children are more likely to want to stay at the shopping centre and have money spent on them, and this makes them valuable to the centre.

It's not possible to support and care about an individual or a group of vulnerable people (whether or not they have a disability, and no matter their age) if you don't see them as having any worth or value – if you don't see that they can contribute in their own unique ways.

In many parts of the world, older people are treated with great respect and are valued for their contribution to the family unit. I once read a story about two sisters' different perspectives of their grandmother, who had dementia. One sister described her grandmother as wonderful company, saying that they both enjoyed going to gardens together. She shared stories from when she was a little girl, saying that she very much looked forward to her weekly visits with her grandmother. The other sister described her grandmother as having already passed away. She said that it was a sad struggle to spend time with her and that she didn't look forward to seeing this person with whom she could no longer communicate.

Perspective is everything. It's like the lenses in your glasses; without the right prescription you can't see well.

Many years ago I had the pleasure of meeting one of the Christian brothers who worked alongside Mother Teresa in India. He said, "In India, when I see someone who is poor, disabled, old and frail, I know how to help them. But here in Australia, with so much material wealth but spiritual poverty, I don't know how to help". Over the years I have often stopped to think about his words and to question why we have an epidemic of lonely, forgotten people living on the edges of our materially wealthy but spiritually bereft culture.

To me, SEPARATION is at the heart of it. We separate into clans of colour, creed, gender and ability, and this cuts each of us off from the bigger part of who we all are. We are just one cell in the body of humanity.

WOUNDS

You only have to spend a small amount of time with most families who have a loved one with a disability to see and feel their wounds. They carry wounds from society's rejection of their loved one. Within a short time of Emma's birth I experienced my first wounds when the medical team did not see the value in trying to prolong her life if she were to crash again. Another wound was inflicted when it was suggested that I could just go home from the hospital and leave her there, with the hospital finding somewhere to put her. Yet another wound occurred a few years later in a small music group when birthday invitations were distributed but Emma was left out. Then there was the mother at the school meeting who called out, "The government's got places for kids like that". On a daily basis I had to hear the very unkind and negative comments of other parents, which were shared in Emma's class through their children.

All of these experiences result in what SRV calls "wounds". The story my father shared of his friend with a brother who had Down syndrome did not result in a wound for my father. However, his fear for Emma's future showed that he held within him a fear of that wounding. His story also illustrates the long history of the devaluation of people with disability in Australia. The woundings I experienced and have shared were very painful, but for some families the wounds are just too much to bear. They feel so hurt and rejected that they are unable or unwilling to see a way to "a good life" for their family member – their faith in humankind has been too badly damaged.

Before I move on to the next chapter I want to say something here about resilience. While resilience is not documented as being part of SRV, I feel it is important to take a moment to acknowledge the important part that resilience plays in all of our lives.

For me, resilience is like water. It can be a quiet tranquil stream that, over many years and merely by its continued presence, gently softens the rough edges of the rocks and stones. The water isn't trying to force the rocks and stones to change. The rocks and stones are changed just by the water constantly running over them. In the same way, resilience is ever-present within us, gently wearing away the rough edges of our wounds.

However, that gentle stream becomes a powerful force when it is in flood. It is then that it can literally move mountains. So it is, too, that when we are hit with an emotional storm, the stream of resilience is transformed into a powerful force within, awaiting our command.

I believe that each of us has resilience as an inherent part of us, in the same way that our hearts keep beating without us having to do anything, and our hair grows without any instruction from us. We are gifted with resilience. It's not something that we have to go to a workshop to get. We don't need to read about it in a book or to sit at the feet of a teacher. It is always there at work for us. However, what we oftentimes *do* lack is the awareness of our resilience. Awareness often the makes difference between success and failure. As I mentioned in the introduction to this book, resilience is like a bank account. Each time we are "pushed" on some front and get through the situation, we put more into our resilience bank account. The secret assistant to resilience is forgiveness. Together, resilience and forgiveness are a powerful force for good.

At the start of this book I shared a very painful and damaging experience with you – namely, being raped and beaten – and the painful shadow it cast over my life for a very long time. The passing of the years has allowed me to see that resilience is what got me through the experience. At times, it carried me when I felt I could no longer stand the pain.

The multiple challenges that Greg and I faced in trying to adopt Laksiri provided many opportunities to withdraw from and deposit into my resilience bank account. Laksiri, himself, is a great example of resilience. He had been left in a large orphanage to starve almost to the point of death, but he held on until I could come and bring him to his new life within a family that loved and wanted him.

I would like to take you back to chapter 14 of this book, where I shared my experiences of working as an advocate for people with disability. The people I met in those houses of horror are great examples of resilience and forgiveness in action. Many of these people had survived all manner of abuse and neglect in large, devaluing institutions. The man I spoke of in a facility who was deaf, and who had spent 30 years – most of his life – unable to have a single conversation with another human being, shows the power of the resilience that is within us all.

Resilience is there with you always, as close as your breath. Or as far as your fear can take you.

CHAPTER 24

My Daughter, the Media Tart (with a Purpose)

"The miracle is never lost. It may touch many people you have not even met, and produce undreamed of changes in situations of which you are not even aware."

— *A Course in Miracles*

One of the key reasons for wanting more funding was so that I could put someone else into the business support role that I had been doing. I felt that it wasn't good for Emma to have me stay in the role. The longer I stayed, the harder it would be for me to get out because Emma would feel that this was how it was always going to be. At the end of the day, Master Shredder is Emma's business – not mine. I knew that Emma needed to make her own way in her role and to determine what kind of boss she wanted to be. I also saw that it's not a good look to have your mum taking you to work.

However, before we received more funding, something pretty amazing happened. One day I got a call from the ABC (the Australian Broadcasting Corporation). One of its local producers had seen a little sign I had placed in a local coffee shop to try to attract more work for Emma. The sign had a photo of Emma and explained her unique service and how she could help local businesses with the disposal of their confidential documents. The producer had spoken to his team about how he thought this might make a good human-interest story. Emma and I met the producer and a journalist and we agreed to do the story. At the time I thought it might help Emma to gain new clients, and it might help another family to see that anything is possible if you look beyond "herd mentality".

I spent considerable time talking to Emma about the upcoming ABC filming, explaining to her that the producer had said they might want to film the same thing from a couple of different angles. I sensed Emma's concern about stepping outside of her comfort zone. So Karen did a brief session with her and reported back to me that, in fact, Emma was picking up on my anxieties. Karen promised to do more work with Emma before the filming.

On the morning of the filming, which was initially at the Queensland Country Credit Union, Emma was an absolute legend (I do wonder if my daughter might be a bit of a "media tart" – when we were doing the photoshoot for the cover of this book the person most at ease in front of the camera was Emma!). She happily followed all of the producer's requests, which included repeating actions while they filmed from a different angle. The ABC then came to our home to interview me and get some footage of Emma in the downstairs flat. Again, Emma was very happy to oblige. Karen later told me that she had talked Emma through the process and pointed out how helpful it would be for people to see the Master Shredder at work. By doing this story she would also be able to help lots of other people just like her, with their families being able to see that they, too, could have a job and go to work.

At the credit union, the HR manager was interviewed. He was asked why the credit union had engaged the services of Master Shredder, and how it was working for them. His responses were insightful and heartfelt. He spoke about how Emma's service was helping them with their need to shred confidential documents, and he said that they had been working for some time on improving diversity within their organisation – they had been very keen to find a way to employ someone with a disability. He then explained that my letter had arrived at the very time that they had been grappling with this issue.

In September the story went up on the ABC's online platform. I thought, "Well, who knows? It might be helpful". A couple of weeks later, that story had generated so much interest that it crashed the ABC site twice. At that point, it had 750,000 hits. The story went all over the globe and was replayed by news outlets all over Europe, the UK, Canada and the US. A television station in Japan contacted the credit union to ask how they had gone about setting things up for Emma. They aired the story on a Sunday evening program in Japan. The story went on to have over a million hits. The first thought that came to me after hearing about the interest it had generated was the comment I had made to the recovery nurse just after Emma was born: "This little girl is not going to be hidden away; you are going to know about her".

I also felt a strong sense of the perfection of things happening just as they are meant to, at the time that has been allotted to them. It was amazing to me that this four-minute story about a young woman with a disability would attract so much interest. Despite the terrible ways in which people with disabilities are so often abused, forgotten and neglected, the story's popularity showed that many people want to see people with disabilities through different eyes. They were open to a young woman changing their minds about what they thought was possible. I also think it was a positive story of hope at a time when so many stories are showing us the very worst of ourselves. We need to see stories of those moments when we are kind for kindness's sake, when we show our capacity for good, and when we demonstrate love – because we have remembered that that is who we are.

The story also had some other unforeseen benefits:

- It had a very powerful influence on Emma. The first time she watched it, she was clearly happy to see herself on TV. She said, "That's me!" But more than that, it gave her a grander sense of who she was. People across the city made comments to her about seeing the story, and this was so gratifying for her.

- I shared the story with Emma's clients, who went on to share it with their family and friends. When her clients told her that they had seen the Master Shredder on TV, it greatly reinforced Emma's feelings of value. It told her that she mattered, and that she was visible. I recall a young receptionist at Mackey Wales Law telling me that she had been on Facebook the night before, and people were talking about the Master Shredder story and sharing it around. This young woman told me with great pride that she had been telling others on Facebook that she worked with Emma, the Master Shredder. That comment told me that Emma belonged and that the team saw her as one of them.

- The story had a wonderful ripple effect throughout our community of families, friends and acquaintances. They, like most of society, had not dreamed that Emma could not only work but could also have her own business and become an inspiration to many people. Family and friends were now seeing Emma as capable and competent, not just as someone who would always need to be cared for. She was seen as being just like any other young woman making her way in the world. They all revealed their immense pride in Emma and in how hard she was working. Even my mum was moved by the story and by who Emma was becoming. She told everyone in the retirement village about her granddaughter, Emma. This is the same granddaughter of whom she had once said would bring shame to the family – and now she was filling my mother with great pride.

The story was used by all kinds of organisations, all over the country, to inspire people to see that anything is possible. A number of disability providers also used it. In fact, the provider we had been with at the time asked if they might use it as part of their training for new staff.

The story – and its success – also had a profound impact on me. This is because it validated what I had said during my role as a community visitor for the justice department. I had said that people's stories *matter*. A person's story shouldn't define who they are, but when told well it helps them to see themselves differently. In turn, it helps others to see them differently. We all have within us a picture, a story, of who we think we are – those around us merely respond to the picture we have of ourselves. So by changing how a person sees and thinks about themselves, it changes the way others see and respond to them.

I became very passionate about having the stories of people with disability told for all to hear. I didn't just want to see these stories on a disability platform like the NDIS site; I also wanted them to be told in mainstream media. For me, this belief was rooted in SRV, because it would be changing the devalued status of a group in the community. We would tell good stories about them, and talk about their loves, their triumphs, their successes and their roles. Through their stories we would show their incredible resilience and courage in the face of the devalued place that society has allotted them. I believe that if we have some control of the narrative about people with disability, it will be an effective way of changing the way the wider community perceives them. It's difficult to ignore someone once you have been shown how much they really are like you, and once you have heard their story.

I wanted stories to be a way for the people of Australia to get to know people with disability and to see them through new eyes – to see them as being a potential friend, a potential co-worker or just a good neighbour. Across all of their platforms, the ABC has been amazing at telling good stories about people with disability. In fact, it has told a number of good local stories on radio. Sadly, the commercial networks are not responding in the same way.

Indigenous people, refugees and elderly people also experience being invisible and devalued. The current narrative about refugees, for example, only shows them as people in need. We don't see the many wonderful gifts and talents that they bring to help enrich our country. If we were to hear about the things that they have achieved and the ways in which they have given back to Australia, we might be more welcoming.

There is another element to changing the narrative about people with disability. A number of years ago I read a fascinating book by Derrick Jensen, called *Truths Among Us*. The book features an interview with George Gerber, who was involved with the Cultural Indicators Project in the US – this project looked at the influence of media on people's lives. George said, "... the telling of all the stories is what makes us develop into who we are; stories teach us our social roles. People who are well represented in stories see many opportunities, many choices. The opposite is true for those who are underrepresented, or are represented only in a particular way. For example, women between the ages of 25 and 35 are generally cast only for romantic roles. What message does that impart to young girls growing up? We have a contract with the Screen Actors Guild to study why so many of its female members stop getting calls when they're 35 and only start getting them again when they are old enough to play grandmothers. What does that invisibility teach women about their roles in society? Men play romantic leads until they totter into their graves. How does that affect people's perception of their opportunities for love, sex and human companionship?"

He goes on to say, "Television has become the universal curriculum. Television and movies project the power structure of our society, and by projecting it, perpetuate it, make it seem normal, make it seem the only thing to do, to talk about, to think about".

I feel that our movies and television shows are like a *social mirror* where young people look to see themselves reflected. In Australia, there was a time not too long ago when there was no representation at all of Aboriginal people on our screens. Slowly, we are seeing and hearing them in movies, TV programs and advertisements.

However, where in the Australian social mirror does a young disabled person see themselves represented? They are rarely featured in TV shows or movies and their presence is almost non-existent in commercials. So, what message is this sending – not just to people with disability, but to the wider community? It says that they are not valuable enough to even be seen. It also perpetuates the misunderstanding that people with disability need their own places, that there is no place for them in the community.

When governments want to change the way people think and behave, the first thing they do is run awareness campaigns. Let's take the example of the campaign to improve the safety of transport department staff who work on busy roads. Firstly, the advertisement told us what the problem was – people driving too fast through worksites. Secondly, it revealed how this behaviour impacts workers – it puts their lives at risk. Thirdly, it demonstrated how we could change our behaviour, which would make those worksites safer. So why did the government spend money on television ads and billboards about safety issues for road workers? Because in order to change behaviour, you must first be aware of it. The aim was to make the road workers "visible" and to show that their role and safety mattered. That is my point here – if a group of people are largely invisible and are not valued, how we can expect the community to respond or engage with them? That group needs to be represented on our screens.

As I said earlier, the exception to the rule here has been the ABC. Commercial media outlets have done little to nothing to promote inclusion (although recently some local outlets have asked me to share different aspects of Emma's story), but the ABC has produced and told many wonderful stories that portray people with disabilities as valued members of the community. It treats their stories as worthwhile. Recently, the ABC even engaged a man with a disability to host one of their regular programs.

The ABC story also resulted in something very unexpected – I started to be asked to speak online and on stage at various disability events. At first I wasn't sure about this, but now I am honoured to be asked to share my amazing daughter's story and more about the journey experienced by people with disabilities (you can see more about this at joannelynam .com/media-speaking).

CHAPTER 25

A New Story Begins

"Change will not come if we wait for some other person or if we wait for some other time. We are the ones we've been waiting for. We are the change that we seek."

— *Barack Obama*

Not too long after the ABC story aired, we managed to secure a little more funding for Emma – this meant we could hire a support worker. We had a lot of discussion about who might be a good fit for Emma and, very importantly, what a good fit would look like. Throughout all of these discussions I felt very grateful for the support of the circle.

Ultimately, the support circle felt it would be best if the person was close in age to Emma. We also decided that Emma and her support worker would have uniforms. A lot of time went into thinking about how to recruit the right person. We placed an advertisement online at the local university and it attracted a lot of applicants, several of whom were foreign students. The support circle was once again a great help because the members' different work backgrounds provided insights into how to go about the interviewing process. A date was set for interviews and this was sent to potential candidates.

We all felt it was important for Emma to be involved in the process of choosing a person to work with her. So we had the interviews downstairs in Emma's space. We had each interviewee sit and watch the ABC story about Emma. This was to give them some idea about the role and who they would be working with. It was also intended to challenge any preconceptions they might have had about what was possible for a person with a disability, and about what it would be like to work with them. The support circle then stepped in to interview each candidate.

There was one young man from India, called Raghu, who stood out to me. Perhaps it was his reaction to the ABC story, or his quiet manner; I am not sure. One of the things that I liked about him was the way he didn't try to sell himself as knowing everything. He acknowledged his limited experience with people with disabilities. Emma was "over" the whole process by the time Raghu sat down, and she was only focused on cooking her dinner. She didn't engage with him at all during the interview. Due to work commitments, Roshan and Laksiri hadn't been able to make it to the interview so I invited Raghu to join us for a family gathering on Sunday afternoon. I felt that in a more relaxed environment with the family, we might get a better idea of what Emma thought about Raghu. When he arrived, Emma was still downstairs. This gave us the opportunity to introduce Raghu to Roshan and Laksiri and to give the boys a chance to ask Raghu some questions that they had. When Emma came upstairs I expected her to sit beside me as she usually did, but no, she chose to sit beside Raghu. Greg and I looked at each other, wondering what had just happened.

The afternoon was very pleasant and Emma indicated, "I like that one". So we offered Raghu the role.

On the Monday morning, Raghu arrived and we chatted a little about what was involved in the role. I suggested that I would drive us to Emma's first client and he could drive home. While Emma was working, Raghu and I had an opportunity to talk more about what was expected of him. I explained that, in most jobs, it's natural to want to "do" everything you can to show that you are a good worker. But in this role your job is more about getting out of the way and encouraging Emma to do more for herself. In this particular instance, if you find yourself doing a lot, you are not doing your job well. I explained that I thought it might take some time for Emma to be ready to let go of working with me and to adjust to working with someone else. I also said that due to the confidential nature of the documents that Emma shreds, you wouldn't be able to have ANY involvement in the shredding. Your job would be to assist Emma by driving her to and from each workplace and helping to her to load and unload the shredder.

Raghu had been working alongside Emma, with my input, for about two weeks when I slept in one morning. When Raghu arrived, I wasn't ready. I apologised to Emma for being late and told her that I would quickly get dressed. She ever so casually looked at me and said, "I am fine. You stay here". I couldn't believe what I was hearing. So off went Emma and Raghu. However, it didn't take Emma long to figure out that Raghu was a gentle soul, and she attempted to exploit that. After just a couple of weeks he told me that Emma would not unload her trolley from the car or put it back in. I had expected this, so the next day I went with them. Sure enough, Emma got out of the car and stood there waiting like a princess for Raghu to do everything for her. I quietly suggested that he just keep walking towards the office. Emma quickly realised that she was going to be left behind, so she got her trolley from the car and walked alongside Raghu. They both worked well together. Raghu was patient and supportive, and very respectful.

As time went by, they sometimes seemed like an old married couple who had little spats and then made up. Having said that, Raghu had a natural easy way of being with Emma. I have no doubt that if she hadn't liked him I would have heard about it. While he worked with Emma, Raghu was also studying and adjusting to a different country and culture. He managed, through all of this, to get distinctions and high distinctions in his study, and he was awarded the academic medal. I am sure his family must be very proud of him. I certainly feel proud of him.

Our decision to employ a young Indian male as Emma's business support worker certainly raised some eyebrows. Deciding to offer Raghu the role came from trusting the feeling in my heart and not listening to the worry in my head. I was focused on finding the best person to work with Emma – it wasn't about their gender or the colour of their skin. I knew that Raghu genuinely cared about Emma and he would never let anything bad happen to her. Of course, he had his own way of managing things when Emma became upset. His process and manner were naturally different from mine, but that was a huge part of why I wanted to get out of the way. It was important that Emma, like all young people, learned to adjust to different kinds of people. ALL young people grow into their roles, in part through the different people who cross their path – that's life. I wanted Emma to know and experience that there is a big world out there, a world way beyond Mum.

I have been asked if Emma might, one day, have another person work within her business. My thinking about this is clear: no, it will not happen. If we invite more people with disability to join Emma in her business, it risks her autonomy and could make the business appear to be some kind

Raghu & Emma

of disability work program. There is also the risk that people will see a group of people with disability shredding and believe that this is what all people with disability will want to do. Shredding is what works for Emma; it should not be seen as a "one size fits all" answer to employment for people with disability.

After I had stepped away from working directly with Emma, initially I felt a bit lost. I missed catching up with her clients. However, having more time to myself allowed me to reflect on where we were now and on what to focus next.

During this time of reflection, Emma and I were asked to present at a symposium. While I was very pleased that Emma and I had been asked to present, Emma was not so pleased. I spoke at length to her about what the day would entail, and mentioned that we would also have the opportunity to catch up with Grandma Lynam and have dinner with her. It was clear that Emma was very anxious about the prospect of standing up in front of a lot of people.

Once again, Karen was very helpful in guiding Emma to see this as a great opportunity. Just as she had done previously, she talked to Emma about the bigger picture. They spoke about the fact that, just by sharing her story with them, Emma would be helping a lot of people to see how they could do things differently. Karen once again came up with creative ways of walking Emma through what the day would entail. In so doing, she helped Emma to see the experience as something that she could manage. Emma understood that she wasn't just helping people by shredding paper – she was now helping people to understand how they could help other people just like her.

On the morning of the symposium, Emma was clearly nervous and uncomfortable about having to stand in front of so many people. As the time approached for us to speak, I quietly mentioned to Emma that I would stand beside her. However, when it came time for Emma to stand up and present, she told me to stay seated. She did her presentation, which was in Pictello on her iPad, and even remembered to sign "thank you". I was amazed at the level of confidence she showed when she stood up to present. It was almost as though the sessions with Karen had lifted a veil from over Emma, allowing her to see herself differently. She then proceeded to heckle me as I was doing my presentation.

I had been asked to share what part I felt I had played in Emma's success. During my presentation I shared a story that I felt was a great example of one of the ways in which I had helped Emma. (Although it's important to understand that this could just as easily be a support worker.) I have included it here, because I feel it is very relevant:

Once upon a time in China there was an emperor who had a very beautiful daughter. The princess was not only beautiful; she was also very intelligent. She was known across the land for her incredible ability to read faces. At this time in China, face-reading was seen as a great art.

The princess spent much time in court with her father, listening to the concerns and issues that were raised with him. She often gave her father sage advice regarding the settlement of a dispute that the emperor had been asked to resolve. The princess would carefully read the various features of each person's face and base her advice upon this.

When the princess reached the age of marriage she suggested to her father that she be allowed to choose her own husband. She reasoned that she was very good by now at reading people's faces and had many times advised her father on a course of action based on a person's face. So she felt she would be able to choose a good husband based upon the characteristics of his face.

A decree went out across the land that the princess was going to choose her own husband. She would choose a handsome man with a kind, gentle and wise face. So as you can imagine every single man under the age of 50 thought he had a shot at marrying the princess.

In a far-off part of the kingdom there was a man who knew the princess would not choose him, with his scarred and crooked face. This man had been a thief and wasn't interested in marrying the princess; he just wanted a way to get into the palace so that he could get his hands on the emperor's money. So he devised a plan. He went to see a mask-maker to have a mask made that portrayed him as handsome, kind and gentle. At that time in China mask-making was a high art.

Finally, the day arrived when the princess would choose her husband. Eligible bachelors had come from far and wide in the hope that the princess would choose them. The man wearing the mask was also there hoping to get his hands on the emperor's money. However, there were armed guards everywhere along the streets keeping a sharp eye on those who wanted the princess's hand in marriage. After waiting all day, the man wearing the mask moved into the palace grounds. Here, there were even more guards with huge swords ready to take off the head of anyone who stepped out of line. He was sweating under the mask, sure that at any moment he would be found out and have his head cut off. He was sure that the mask would slip off and his deceit would be discovered.

At last, there he was in front of the princess. "She is beautiful", he thought to himself. However, by that stage he didn't want to marry her; he just wanted to get out of the palace alive. The princess spoke kindly to him and said, "What a kind and gentle face you have". What? He thought, "How can this be?" The princess announced that she would marry him. He felt sure he was about to be found out and would lose his head. He told the princess he was just a simple man who was not worthy of her.

The princess said she knew this would be a big adjustment for him, so she gave him one year to think about his decision. He was told that he should come back one year to the day to tell her what he had decided.

Well, the poor man shot out of there, thinking he would get as far away as he could. However, there was a problem. Everyone in the palace knew that he was the one the princess had chosen. So he couldn't take off the mask or he would lose his head. He went back to his village, where everyone now knew that he was the one the princess had chosen. People began knocking on his door to ask him questions, but instead of yelling at them to go away (which he would have done before), he had to stop and try to think of something nice to say.

Day after day the man had to get up and put on the mask and pretend to be gentle and kind to people. He had to remind himself constantly to remember to say kind things and use a gentle tone. But after some time the man began to notice that he liked people speaking to him so respectfully. He liked that people came to him with their problems, seeking his help. Most of all, he really liked the way he felt. He liked that people asked him for his opinion and to help resolve disputes. They even asked him to name their children.

As the day drew closer for him to return to the palace and give the princess his answer, he knew he could not lie to the princess. He was no longer that sort of person. He decided to tell the princess the truth, no matter if it meant that he lost his head. He could not lie.

When finally he and the princess were alone, he confessed the truth: he wasn't a kind and gentle man – he had simply wanted a way to get into the emperor's treasury so that he could steal his money. The princess was shocked, but she didn't want him to be killed. So she said he could go. Just as he was about to leave, the princess asked him to remove the mask and show her his real face. Slowly the man began to remove the mask from his face, waiting to hear the princess gasp. Instead, the princess looked puzzled and said, "Why you would have a mask made in the exact likeness of your own face?" The man said, "What? Could you please show me a mirror?" The princess held up a mirror so that the man could see his face. He could not believe what he was seeing; his once-crooked, scarred face now looked exactly like the mask he had been wearing for the past year.

He had become a kind, gentle and caring person. Where once his disregard for others showed in his crooked, scarred face, now his care and kindness towards others had changed him from the inside out.

The point of sharing this story with you is to show that, much like the thief in the story, I had encouraged Emma to wear the mask of a successful young businesswoman. In the beginning, just like the man in the mask, Emma did not feel like the person I was telling her she was. However, over time she saw the respect and admiration that others had for her. Just like the man in the mask, she liked what she was experiencing and so she began to see herself as a successful young businesswoman. She became the Master Shredder. When we choose to take on an identity, we start to embody it. So why not choose an empowered identity for ourselves and encourage the loved ones in our lives to do the same?

Earlier in this book I mentioned that when I was a young musician I just loved the feeling of playing music. I have always felt that music is part of the world of the magical and the mystical. Whether you are writing, playing or just enjoying music, it means that you have tapped into something far greater than yourself – into the divine part of you called your imagination (this can happen with any art form, but for me it was music). It was my imagination that helped me in the early days of the Master Shredder business. I used it to see and feel what a bright future Emma had, a future that was just waiting for her to reach out and take it.

CHAPTER 26

Do It Anyway

"Only those who will risk going too far can possibly find out how far one can go."

— *TS Eliot*

Emma had been living downstairs for about 18 months when I started thinking about her next big step – moving her into a place of her own. It had been wonderful to see her confidence soar as a result of living independently within our home, but I cast my vision well into the future. What would happen to her confidence if she still lived here when Greg and I passed away? She might feel as though she was losing everything that mattered to her – her parents *and* her home. So I began to seriously consider that next step...

I need to point out that I had very real concerns about this. When the thought, "Emma needs to move out and into the world" originally came to me, I felt a wave of fear, like an undercurrent threatening to pull me under. It was a fear of all of the things that I imagined could go wrong. I quickly recognised that this fear belonged to me and my past and had no place in Emma's life. So, right there, I did something very unusual. I didn't run from the fear. Instead, I stared into it and faced it down by starting to plan for how Emma might move out, and to where. I told myself that Emma's life is not mine; it is hers, and she doesn't need my fear holding her back. While I love Emma more than life itself, and I know that she loves me, I REALLY had to let her go out into the world. As I sat in my lounge room staring down my fears, I could hear all of the voices of concern whispering, "What if something happens to her?" My answer was, "What if she stays here and nothing happens FOR her?"

I wasn't sure how to approach the subject with Emma. Obviously, I didn't want her to feel as though she was being pushed out of home, but I was certainly keen to get her used to the idea of living in her own place. So one Saturday I looked online for upcoming "open houses". I made note of four properties that we could get to over a period of several hours. I took Emma to see units and houses – it didn't really matter what type of property they were. At that stage I was just planting seeds. When we entered each property we started off by merely walking around. Then, we would go back and look at the kitchen, and I would suggest that it could be a nice kitchen to cook in. We would head to the living area and I'd say, "What a great place to sit and watch DVDs". When wandering around a bedroom, I'd say, "This is a really lovely bedroom. It has lots of room". I didn't say anything about Emma moving out. We did this for about six weeks, and took photos of Emma looking at the different properties. These photos then went onto her iPad so that she could show her colleagues what she had been up to on the weekend. However, more support would be needed before we could think about Emma moving into a place of her own.

I consulted with the support circle, understanding that the idea of Emma living independently was a huge leap for them. I presented them with lots of examples of other families having done the same thing, and asked for their support on this new adventure. The members were very good at brainstorming and generated ideas about this next big step – they also asked great questions such as: is it safe? What safeguards need to be put in place? Who can help us? Have you thought about this or that? The questions and discussions that came up in the support circle were like gold to me, because each one challenged my thinking and gave me a fresh perspective. Members also discussed Emma's lack of support staff funding and how that was holding her back from living independently. It was decided that I would write to Queensland Disability Services to see what could be done about getting more funding. I spent a lot of time going backwards and forwards but, in the end, Lorna again helped us to secure more funding.

I realised, too, that I would have to start to step back out of Emma's life so that I could eventually take myself right out of the picture. I began with considering how to remove myself from the now very-routine pattern of Emma's mornings. I had a person in mind to replace me. I had only recently caught up with this person for Christmas drinks, so I asked her if she might be interested in taking on the role of supporting Emma in the mornings. There was no way of knowing how Emma would greet this next new step in her life, but we agreed to head in the direction of independent living and invite Emma to step up to her next big adventure.

Initially I told Emma that I had a very early morning meeting and that therefore Kylie would come to help her get ready for work. Right from the first morning, Emma was comfortable with Kylie and looked forward to her coming. In fact, Emma was much more cooperative with Kylie than with me. Eventually I just stayed upstairs and Emma was happy with Kylie helping her.

Kylie and Emma really had a quite magical and instant connection. Kylie understood and quickly embraced the idea of offering Emma opportunities that reflect what's "typical" for any young person of the same age (see my perspective on this SRV concept in chapter 23), so the two of them began to explore different areas of Emma's life. Kylie also appreciated the support circle's vision of a rich and meaningful life for Emma.

One of the areas I was keen for Emma to explore was religion/spirituality. I was conscious of the fact that while I don't embrace any religion, this should not determine or decide what Emma might gain from being involved in a religious organisation. I did take Emma to a couple of conventional churches but she clearly wasn't interested. I then heard about a particular church that Emma might enjoy going to because it attracted a lot of young people and had a pretty funky rock program. I thought this church might offer opportunities for involvement because it had a youth group, and this could be a helpful way for Emma to meet other young people. I spoke with a team member about Emma doing some voluntary work for the Sunday evening program. Emma was offered the role of welcoming people to the evening service. At that point I stepped back and let Kylie take her. Emma eventually decided that, while she enjoyed the music, there was too much talking and she wasn't interested in the discussions, so she stopped going.

It seems that Kylie had come into our lives for another reason, too. We had no idea of where we should look for a place for Emma but, just like everything else in life, when we let go, the answer shows up. Kylie was living in the city and told us that there was a unit available for rent in the complex where she was living. It had a lot of things going for it, including the fact that there were only six units in the complex. I thought it would be good for Emma to have a small number of neighbours (in this case it would be just five other people or couples), as this would make it easy for her to form some kind of relationship or connection with them. I was relieved that such an ideal situation seemed to have fallen into our lap.

CHAPTER 27

Letting Go

"Take small steps and achieve big things."

— *Tao Te Ching*

To begin with, Kylie took Emma to look at the unit and to ask the question, "What do you think about living here?" Emma was unsure. She was a bit thrown by the concept of moving away from Mum and Dad. Greg and I went to look at the property. It had just one bedroom, with a small niche for a laundry, but the unit was a good size for one person and the rent was reasonable. We made the decision to sign a 12-month lease that day.

I knew we would have to proceed slowly with Emma so that she didn't feel as though she was being kicked out of home. It was important for her to want to move, to see the benefits. Greg and I took Emma several times to see the unit and although she liked the idea of being closer to Kylie, she seemed a bit puzzled by it all. Kylie spoke to the other residents in the complex (as did I) about Emma moving in. They were very supportive. We took Emma to meet the different residents at different times, and we were constantly talking to her about how exciting it would be for her to move out of home. On Fridays after Emma had finished her shopping, Rebekah would drive her past the unit. She would talk with Emma about moving out of Mum and Dad's place and how wonderful it would be for her. Still, Emma was not on board. Then I suddenly realised that we were taking Emma to look at an empty unit. It made sense that she didn't understand why we would want her to live in an empty home. In the meantime, Kylie decided to plan a house-warming party for Emma. She would invite the other residents to come along and get into the spirit of Emma moving in. We felt that the day of the party would be a good day to set as the move-in day.

Karen had done some initial work with Emma around the idea of her moving out, and she reported back to me that she had a strong sense that making the place pretty – with lots of bright colours – would be very helpful because it would be more appealing to Emma. So rather than use furniture Emma already had in our downstairs room, Greg and I set out to get some bright, colourful new furniture and curtains to make her new home look great. (Emma had won a local award – The John McDonald IGA Community Achievement Award – for her achievements in the community, and she received $1000 as part of that. This came in handy when we were decorating the unit.) We decided not to take Emma back to the unit until the makeover was complete – she would then have a wonderful surprise when she opened her front door. I must say, I had a lot of fun finding bright, fun, funky things for the unit. In the end, I would have been happy to have moved in myself.

I rang Karen to ask her to work with Emma once again so that I could get some sense of how she was really feeling about the move. Karen told me later that while she worked with Emma she spoke with her about Roshan and Laksiri no longer living at home. She said that that is what young adults do; they move into their own place. Karen was very creative in using characters from *Glee* to illustrate that she was a lot like the young characters who were moving on with their lives. She also talked to Emma about the enormous amount of learning and growth she had already experienced from other changes in her life, and that this change would do the same for her. She would be becoming more of a woman.

The day after Karen's session was Saturday, which was the party day. Emma was very happy about going to the unit for the party. Kylie had gone to great lengths to make sure that the unit looked lovely, with candles and flowers everywhere. When Emma walked in and saw the transformation from an empty unit to a colourful beautiful home where any young woman would want to live, she was clearly very pleased. When she saw the new double bed we had bought for her, with its pretty bedspread, she was very happy – a big bed all to herself was apparently a game-changer. I lay back on the bed and she quickly told me, "No, Mum, not you. That's mine".

The party was a lot of fun and everyone enjoyed themselves, especially Emma. In the lead-up to the party, I had talked to Emma about her moving into the unit in gradual steps over a period of time. She could stay there during the week and come home to us on the weekend. The following morning was Sunday. Emma and I went to the markets as we usually did, and then went back to the unit. We relaxed, had lunch and discussed how she would do her washing and where she would dry things at the unit. I was ready to go home by mid-afternoon, but to my surprise Emma said she would stay and watch a DVD. So I went home and came back later with some dinner, fully expecting that Emma would return home with me that night. After she finished dinner, I said that it was time to go home; however, she looked at me from her lovely green lounge and calmly said, "No, I stay here". I clarified this with her several times to be sure that I was understanding her. I said, "So you want to have a shower here and sleep here tonight?" She kept repeating, "Yes, I stay here". I was beyond thrilled, and thought to myself that it couldn't be that easy.

What I hadn't calculated was the sudden rise of fears that would come over me at the moment of actually letting go. I kissed her goodnight and told her how proud I was of her. I then left the unit. As I pulled the front door closed behind me, I felt shaky and weak all over. I sat on the step and began to cry, with a wild rush of emotions racing through me. Initially I felt paralysing fear, with my mind suddenly full of all of the things that could possibly go wrong. After 20 minutes I pulled myself together and let Kylie know I was going home. Backing the car out of the parking space and driving away was so tough. I cried for most of the 20-minute drive home. The plan for Emma to come home on the weekends never happened; she loved her new life in the unit.

Almost immediately after moving to the unit, Emma began to embrace her independence by taking responsibility for taking her rubbish out to the wheelie bin. She had never done this at home so it was good to see her taking this on. She was wanting to make more decisions and accept the consequences, but sometimes this resulted in her experiencing a tough lesson (but an important one – for example, at one stage she started sleeping in, and this resulted in her starting work later and missing afternoon tea because the shop had closed). Without any prompting, when she finished work on Monday afternoon she would take her washing off the line and put it away. In many ways, Emma is no different to any other young person moving out of home. She certainly pushed boundaries to see just how far she could go, letting everyone know that, in this space, "I am the boss". She also took great pride in the appearance of the unit; many

Initially I felt paralysing fear, with my mind suddenly full of all of the things that could possibly go wrong.

times Greg or I would get into trouble for leaving something out on the bench, or for leaving a cup on the coffee table. Emma would glare at us and put things where they were supposed to be.

I started thinking about small ways in which Emma could engage with her neighbours. One of the things I encouraged her to consider was that she could do something nice for each of the neighbours. After she moved into the unit she began asking her support staff to take her to the flower shop each week to buy fresh flowers (she let everyone know that she really liked flowers in her home) – and sometimes she would also buy some for Kylie. It was very satisfying to see Emma embracing and enjoying her new independent life. While we were at the markets one Sunday Emma wanted to get some bananas, so I suggested that she might like to buy some for the man who lived downstairs. She then began to think each week about whether she would buy fruit or flowers for her neighbours. This simple act of kindness was much appreciated by her neighbours.

Living in the city meant that Emma was now close to Townsville's nightlife. As I mentioned earlier, Emma and Kylie had a really great relationship, and Kylie knew that we wanted Emma to have the opportunity to experience all that life had to offer. Kylie and Emma went to local bars and restaurants where Emma got to enjoy live bands and even meet the band. Who knew that Emma liked a beer or a glass of bubbly? Not me! She explored different foods and concerts and met new people. Kylie also encouraged Emma to work on her fitness, which led to Emma trying her hand at martial arts. A neighbour downstairs offered for Emma to practise her kicks and punches with him and Kylie encouraged this – Emma really enjoyed these sessions because her neighbour would put on music while they practised.

As Christmas drew near we talked about Emma hosting Christmas drinks for her neighbours. I have always felt it's important to get to know who are your neighbours and how you might be able to help each other. This keeps us connected and safe. Having Emma's neighbours know and engage with her was important for helping to keep her safe.

The Christmas party was a really lovely night, with Emma's neighbours all popping in for a drink and something to eat. One of the neighbours kept us entertained with stories about some of the goings-on of previous tenants. Driving home that night after the party, feeling tired but happy, I thought about what had made it was such a good night – it was getting to know these people a little more and realising that it was the first time they had ever come together. They had previously only ever just said "hello" in the hallway. Emma offered them a way to come together and to get to know each other as more than just "the person in number three". Although it had taken a lot of time and effort to touch base with the neighbours before Emma moved in, it was worth it. They all cared about Emma and she also cared about them. There also came to be other opportunities for socialising with this lovely group of people – when someone had a birthday, they would go out for a meal together.

I remember lying in bed after the Christmas party, thinking about all the people I had met in group homes and the lives they were forced to submit to. I thought about the fact that they had no control over their lives. I could see their faces and imagine them living in a place just like Emma, with them getting to make choices about simple things such as what to eat, where they want to live and whether or not they want to share their space with anyone. Emma was, essentially, like so many of the people in group homes, in that she had Down syndrome and autism and was deaf. However, her life was a million miles away from theirs – because she had real choice.

CHAPTER 28

Get Up & Go On

*"Everything in life happens for a reason.
There are no accidents... just life's unfolding."*

— *Joanne Lynam*

About a month after Emma had moved into the unit she was really quite settled and happy. Late one Friday afternoon, after I'd been shopping, I decided to pop in to say "hi" to Emma. As soon as I opened the door, I knew something was wrong. She wasn't watching her DVDs. She was lying on the floor in front of the bathroom. My heart sank as I rushed to her. She was crying and signing, "Hurting, hurting". After I got her up off the floor it was clear she had fallen and hurt her arm – she couldn't move it. I phoned for an ambulance. At the hospital, they examined her arm and did an X-ray, telling me that her arm wasn't broken and that we could go home. However, in my heart I knew it was broken. I don't know how I knew, but I did. On the Monday morning I took Emma to our GP and he gave instructions for the way another X-ray was to be done. This new X-ray showed that her arm was not only broken – a piece of bone had broken off. She would need surgery to repair and pin the bone.

After Emma's fall there was a lot of talk about her not being able to remain in the unit. The support circle was concerned about the potential risks of Emma living independently, and it was felt that we should possibly bring Emma home to live with us. My only focus at the time was on getting Emma through the surgery and recovery; then we could talk about what was to happen next. Emma only stayed overnight in hospital. The next morning she insisted on going back to the unit, but within a short time she wasn't feeling well. She reluctantly agreed to come back home with me, no doubt only because she was vomiting due to the medication. We gave her some medication for the vomiting, and she then slept right through to the next morning (about 15 hours). The following morning Emma insisted on going back to the unit; she wasn't prepared to negotiate. I took some clothes and slept on the floor for a couple of nights. When Greg came back from his time away working he also slept there for a night. Emma then put her foot down and threw us both out, telling us, "I am fine".

The first couple of weeks after the surgery I spent most of each day with her, taking her out for morning tea and drives along the beach. By the third week she was bored silly, so I asked Raghu to take her to visit all of her clients so she that could have a chat and show off her "injury". This did get her a lot of attention, which she lapped up. In the fourth week Emma and Raghu repeated this, with one difference – Emma said to all of her clients, "I will see you next week", making it clear that she would be back at work. When Raghu told me about this I was concerned. I spoke to the surgeon about her going back to work so soon. He felt that if that was what she wanted to do, it should be fine. It turned out to be the best thing for her recovery. She wasn't too keen on doing the exercises her physiotherapist had recommended because she didn't want to use her injured arm, but by being back at work she forgot about her arm and started using it normally.

As I mentioned, after Emma's fall there had been a lot of discussion about her continuing to live in the unit. There was felt to be a need to mitigate future risk. As far as I was concerned, it was her decision to make – by staying in the unit after her injury she had shown great courage and determination. I discussed with Emma some of the concerns that others had about her safety, in regards to living in the unit on her own. However, Emma rightfully had the final say, and chose to stay. Emma's decision to remain in the unit told me that she was loving her life of independence and that she was a lot stronger than any of us thought. It also showed me that shit happens to all of us but it doesn't have to be the end of us. Yes, she fell, but she got back up and wanted to get on with HER life.

There is great dignity in risk, particularly for a person with a disability. Very often their lives are risk assessed to such an extent that they are left with no real life to enjoy or explore. The first time we as parents take a child out to teach them how to ride a bike there is the risk that they might fall off and break something. But there is also the chance that they will learn to get their balance and ride off to independent adventures under their own steam. This gives them the gift of self-confidence. It instills in them the knowledge that they can learn new things and acquire new skills and that life is a constant learning process. That tiny seed of self-confidence will grow and be there to serve them throughout their life. There are always risks with every decision that we make, but beyond the risk is the opportunity to create, learn something amazing and soar to new heights.

At the end of the day, if your attention is focused on the fear of what might happen, you can be sure it will happen – because that's where you invested your energy.

CHAPTER 29

Up, Up & Away

"Be brave enough to live the life of your dreams
according to your vision and purpose instead of
the expectations and opinions of others."

— Roy T Bennett

One of the goals for 2017 was for Emma to have another holiday, but this time it would be overseas to Japan. Emma was very keen to see Disneyland in the US, but we felt that the trip might be too long for her. Japan was closer and it still had Disneyland. Despite having broken her arm and undergone surgery, Emma was still very keen to press on with the plans for her and Rebekah to go to Japan in September, just after her birthday.

The support circle members were absolutely invaluable in the lead-up to the trip. Each member of the circle brought so many insights, ideas and great questions to the table in planning an overseas holiday for a person with a disability. They looked into how she would be able to phone us

– Emma prefers to use FaceTime when she calls so that she can see and sign to me. What would need to be in place for Emma to be able to communicate via FaceTime? What costs would be involved? What would be the best way for her to carry money and what was the most cost-effective way to manage this?

Members also asked how we could plan for anything going wrong while they were in Japan. Who had a contact there who might be willing to lend a hand, if needed? For this, we asked a nephew of the local theatre company's front-of-house coordinator (Emma had done volunteer work at this company). He was more than willing to provide support. The circle also had the great idea to find someone who had recently been to Japan so that we could ask them questions about local issues. There were other concerns, too – Emma had never been on a plane for nine hours before. How would she manage this? How would she understand or cope with the toilets on a plane? Her previous trips to Brisbane with me, and to the Gold Coast with Rebekah, were two-hour flights. But within the nine hours to Japan, she would have to go to the toilet at some point. The support circle members were absolute champions in helping us to plan and to prepare Emma for the trip.

In the lead-up to the trip, I had a lot of concerns and anxieties. My way of managing this was to ask Karen to work with Emma and help prepare her for the trip. Karen told me that the way she approached the Japan trip was to show Emma that this was something else that young adults do – they go on overseas holidays. My biggest concern was how Emma would manage the nine hours on a plane. Karen's ability to think outside the square paid off once again. For this flight, Karen was aware that Emma would be taking her iPad, and that it had a number of movies on it for her to watch. So Karen talked with Emma about the length of each of her movies, and how many movies she would be able to watch on the flight to Japan. She also talked with her about how many meals she might have. All of this was fascinating to Emma. The support circle also worked hard to problem-solve any potential issues.

On the day that they flew out for Japan, Emma yet again revealed great resilience and determination in the face of her own anxiety. She was very excited about going on the holiday, but as the moment of departure arrived I could see her anxiety rising. This was no doubt brought on by the thought of separating from Mum and Dad. Her way of managing this was to get up and walk beside Rebekah down the tunnel and onto the plane without saying goodbye – or even looking at – Greg or me. I felt that if she stopped to kiss us goodbye she wouldn't be able to let herself leave.

Emma had a fantastic time in Japan and loved every minute of it. After all of the effort that had gone into ensuring that she would be able to FaceTime us, she didn't call us. Not once. Fortunately for me, Rebekah was sending regular photos and updates, so I knew that Emma was alright.

With all of the detailed planning and organisation that was needed for Emma to go to Japan, it would be easy to question why we did it. The answer? Because going overseas is something that lots of young people do; it's typical (remember this concept from SRV in chapter 23?). Overseas travel offers them the opportunity to be immersed in a different culture, to see different things and to view the world from a different perspective. It opens and broadens their minds. The greatest lessons for all of us appear when we get out of our comfort zones. The really big thing that I was keen for Emma to realise was that she can experience all kinds of things without her family. I wanted her to know that it's fine for her to enjoy her life without us, just like any other young person.

One of the places that we had booked for Emma to visit was Tokyo's Robot Restaurant. It was suggested that it might be a bit too loud and intense for Emma, but I decided to let

Rebekah & Emma having a ball at Disneyland, Japan

her go and see what happened. I reasoned that if she didn't like it, she didn't have to stay. It ended up being a big hit with Emma, and is one of her favourite memories of the trip.

Rebekah told me that she was really proud of the way Emma got up each day and just embraced whatever the day had to offer, including a trip on the Tokyo rail (though not in peak hour!).

A few weeks after Emma came back from Japan, Kylie took her to Brisbane to see Cirque du Soleil and to see Grandma Lynam, who was very frail and didn't have much time left. Emma and Grandma had a very beautiful last visit – Grandma passed away not long after. I felt it was important for Emma to experience this time with her grandmother and to have an understanding that Grandma would die.

During my time with the justice department I saw so often that people with a disability were completely left out of the process of the death of a loved one. In fact, I have a very lasting memory of a site I visited one day where a woman came out of her room saying, "Mum, Mum". She was then distressed to see me and not her mum. When I asked staff about this, they explained that her mother had died several years ago and that she was still very raw and sad about her mother no longer being here with her. When staff and management choose not to include the person with a disability in the dying and funeral process of a loved one, I am sure they feel they are sparing the person from the pain and grief they would feel at the loss of their loved one. But it doesn't do that at all. In fact, it creates anxiety in the person with a disability because they are left wondering where their loved one has gone and why they don't see them anymore. Death is simply another part of life, so if we want a person to have a full and rich life then surely this must mean that ALL of life is to be experienced – whether those experiences be bitter or sweet.

CHAPTER 30

Many Hands of Help

*"Every moment of your life is infinitely creative
and the universe is endlessly bountiful. Just put forth
a clear enough request, and everything your
heart desires must come to you."*

— *Mahatma Gandhi*

Towards the end of 2017 a number of support circle members moved on to different things in their lives. I was contemplating how to go about inviting new members when I heard about a concept called "microboards". A microboard is a bit like a support circle but it has a more formal structure. Greg and I attended a workshop to find out more about how and why they work. We both liked the fact that the board ultimately becomes an incorporated body that exists to provide more support for the person with a disability. A microboard would also provide a way for us to plan, and put in place structures, for when Greg and I are no longer here. The thing that really appealed to me about having a microboard was that it could also help to coordinate support services for a person with a disability, as well as creating and fostering their friendships and employment opportunities.

The NDIS offers families the chance to self-manage funding for their loved one's supports. I have self-managed Emma's NDIS funding from the point at which she entered the scheme. However, I liked the idea of having a group of supportive and committed people to help manage the funding. Building a supportive team around Roshan and Laksiri was also very important to me. I wanted to make sure that, after Greg and I have passed on, they feel comfortable taking on the responsibility of not just managing Emma's funding but also being able to secure it in the first place. Having a board in place now affords the boys time to grow into their roles, all while being supported. I really like the fact that microboards are based on the principles of SRV and that they have a strong focus on self-determination.

I was also very keen on the idea of having the microboard as the formal employer of Emma's staff. This would not only relieve some of the pressure on me; it would also make it much better for staff. A microboard would be able to support the recruitment process for new staff.

One of the big benefits of a microboard over a support circle is that the microboard has legal teeth. As an incorporated organisation you can apply for grants, which can't be done with a support circle. Of course, it also has more responsibility – one being the need to have an annual audit. It must also have a constitution and formal meeting guidelines, and meeting minutes must be taken and kept.

We made the decision to form a microboard for Emma. Microboards Australia helped us with all areas of establishing the board, including determining who to invite to be members, and how to invite them. This organisation also helped to clarify the vision for Emma, and provided a great

deal of support around what to document in the recommended Podio app. This app allows you to run your projects
and/or organisation and collaborate with your team re-
motely. The ultimate aim was for Podio to record everything
the board or staff might need to know about Emma and how
to support her.

To that end, we began to record the 80-plus signs that
Emma uses; some of the signs are unique to her. This has
been a simple matter of using an iPhone to video the signs
while Emma is signing them. We have also recorded how
to support Emma if she is upset and how to help her make
decisions – again, we have recorded some examples as
short videos. We have also detailed what to look for if there
is a problem with her ears. To this end, we documented the
history of ear problems that resulted in Emma requiring
a graft on her right eardrum. This history helps staff to
understand why it's important to act quickly if there is
any concern about Emma's ears, and to know what action
needs to be taken. We wanted to create a comprehensive
document that we can leave behind so that those entrusted
with Emma's care have a road map for helping her to
continue going forward.

To help you more deeply understand the microboard
concept, I've created an analogy that also explains why
families can benefit from having one in place. When people
are designing and constructing a building with a large roof
area, the weight of the roof isn't loaded onto just one pole.
The weight is spread over many beams to ensure that it
doesn't collapse. That's what a microboard does – it spreads
the weight over many people so that it's not just the family
carrying the load.

Over the years I have met hundreds of parents who have
a son or daughter with a disability. No matter where the
conversation begins, it usually ends with, "I worry about
what will happen when I am not here". I could not count the

*... it spreads the weight
over many people so that
it's not just the family
carrying the load.*

number of nights on which I have lain in bed worrying about what might happen to Emma when I'm gone. It's often the little things that cause the greatest amount of angst, such as, "Who will be there to comfort her? How will people know why she only likes to wear certain clothes? Who will know what makes her happy and how to help her when she is upset?" Now that Emma's Master Shredder business is doing well, it adds another dimension to the need for future planning. Business information needs to be shared and not just stored in my head. I also want recorded the ideas that I have to help Emma in her growth – the many and varied ways for her to experience life.

It's always difficult to ask people to join you in a venture like a microboard. It's all voluntary and has legal responsibilities, so often the first thought we have is, "Oh, I can't ask someone to help me with my loved one; no one will want to give up their time for this". What I came to learn about this flawed thinking was that it came from a place within me of, "I can do this myself" and "I want to be independent". But the truth is, we all depend on each other for so many of our daily needs. For example, I can't make bread – I have tried. I totally suck at it, so I depend on others to produce the bread for me. I also suck at sewing, so I need others to produce clothes for me. I may need a doctor whose skills I don't have, and on and on it goes. Understanding and being grateful for our interconnectedness makes us stronger.

We've been able to reduce our bureaucratic paperwork load substantially because of the microboard. For example, back in 2013 Emma and I had gone to the bank to open an account into which her pension could be paid. However, the bank advised us that because Emma had an intellectual impairment, she was deemed as not having the capacity to manage a bank account in her own name. The bank's legal department advised us that we would need to apply to be Emma's legal guardians. As far as I was concerned, this was just madness. So Greg and I sought further legal advice and were told that applying to be Emma's guardian was our only option.

Completing the guardianship application requires a lot of patience because the level of bureaucratic crap is unbelievable. After submitting the mountain of paperwork to begin the process, each year a financial report has to be sent through, including a copy of every bank statement for the year. If you have withdrawn $500 or more there must be an explanation, as well as receipts for this expenditure. Then, every five years, a comprehensive report needs to be submitted, and it is to include a medical report. Needless to say, we were very much against going down this route but we really didn't have a choice.

By 2018 Greg and I had done a lot of work to set up the microboard, which will care for Emma (her business, her NDIS funding, her staff and her property) after we have gone. We felt that the microboard would be a more appropriate fit than a support circle. Also, by that time I was tired of being treated like a second-class citizen every time I had to deal with the department that was in charge. The microboard's members knew and cared about Emma and they were invested in her life, whereas the government bureaucrats wouldn't even speak to you without you giving them a client number. We requested a review in November 2018, with the aim being that the microboard would take over the responsibilities that the bureaucrats in the Office of the Damned were doing. However, our request was knocked back because the microboard was not yet incorporated. Our guardianship was extended for another 12 months.

As November 2019 drew closer we prepared for another review. Each review is done at the local courthouse – just to add a further layer of humiliation to the whole process, you have to sit in a courtroom with the member perched up high, looking down at you. For this review we were well organised. We had a letter from our doctor advising that Emma was capable of appointing an enduring power of attorney. For families wanting to get away from guardianship, this step with the doctor is an important one. I was well aware that a doctor could not sign a document stating that the person had capacity if he or she wasn't convinced that the person did indeed have it.

To prepare Emma for independence with money, I started to talk with her about it. I started by asking her what she thought money was for. She answered by signing, "Going for morning tea and having cake and chocolate milk. Going to the movies and out to restaurants". This told me that she did have a basic understanding of money's purpose. She also explained that she could use cash by taking some out of her purse and she could also pay for things by pulling out her card. Next, I took her to the credit union and asked a staff member to speak with Emma about her money and where it was. Then I expanded this conversation to include Greg, Roshan and Laksiri, with them talking to her about working to get money and what they used their money for. My next step was to include staff in this conversation.

When I felt Emma was ready to see the doctor so that he could determine whether or not she had capacity with money, we booked an appointment. However, at that first appointment Emma just sat and refused to answer his questions about money. More work was needed. On our second appointment Emma very clearly answered the doctor's first question about where Emma's money was. She took out some cash and her card to show him. When he asked her what she used money for, she explained that she used her card to buy DVDs, go to the movies, go out for morning tea and go out to dinner. He then asked her if anyone helped her with her money and she said, "Yes, Mum". His final question was, "Who else could help you with your money if Mum was unable to?" Emma signed, "Roshan and Laksiri". With that, the doctor was absolutely certain that Emma did, indeed, have an understanding of her money. He happily signed the letter stating that, in his opinion, Emma had the capacity to appoint a power of attorney over her financial affairs.

In the lead-up to the review, I asked members of the microboard to come along on the day. We took four members of the microboard with us, as well as a staff member to support Emma (should she want to use her iPad to communicate with the member undertaking the review). Prior to the review I had also been reading the United Nations' *Convention on the Rights of Persons with Disabilities*. In particular, I was looking for references to people's rights around their financial affairs and guardianship.

The morning of the review, there were nine of us there for Emma. We outnumbered the bureaucrats in a considerable way. I had done this quite deliberately, just to balance the scales a little – namely, our nine verses their two perched up on high. However, the member was very interested in the microboard and welcomed the chance to ask questions of its members. He also very much appreciated Emma choosing to share her stories with him. In the end, the member said that he was very happy to revoke the guardianship order. He said he thought that the microboard was a good alternative to guardianship, and he wished us well. With that, we were free from the chains of the Office of the Damned.

Here are the reasons I believe the order was revoked:

- The member being open to, and interested in, the idea of guardianship being replaced by a microboard formed around a person with a disability

- Having members of the board there at the review hearing to answer questions about their role and why they are on the board

- The letter from the doctor advising that Emma was able to appoint an enduring power of attorney

- Emma making the choice to share stories of her life with the member. From the moment Emma indicated that she had something to say, it was clear that the member was very interested in hearing from her. He was clearly very happy when Emma shared stories about her holidays with him. It's really important that people in positions of great authority, like that of the member at the review hearing, have an opportunity to GET TO KNOW the person whose life they are holding in the balance.

- My researching of the role and power of the member, and of the impact of any decision they made (ie, whether or not we would have the right to appeal)

- Understanding what the member was expecting of us

Microboards are a fantastic concept and, as you can imagine, I highly recommend them. Here are some examples of their power. In late November 2019, we had to look for a new staff member because another staff member was moving out of town. The microboard gathered to discuss the four applicants who had sent their resumes to us. On the following day the board would interview the candidates. One board member came up with the idea of asking each candidate if he could film them. This was so that we could show the interviews to Emma, allowing her to give her input and see each candidate. He asked each candidate to say something to Emma, and he then sent the videos to the iPad.

That afternoon, Emma showed the videos to the staff member who was leaving. Emma then shared them with yet another staff member. To see this level of maturity in her was, of course, wonderful – however, my point is that this board member gave Emma a great opportunity to share this change in her life with other people. In so doing, it helped her to adjust to having a new person come into her life. The next morning I opened my emails to find that the treasurer had sent a clear plan for the next steps for the microboard to take before offering the position to the young person we had chosen. The contributions made by these board members are great examples of the "load-sharing" benefits of a microboard.

At a recent board meeting, one of the members suggested that we look at the roles of members and allocate tasks that make the most of each member's skillsets. One particular board member shared with me that, until we did this, he had not quite understood what his role was. He helped me to see the importance of each member having a sense of ownership for some part of the running of the board. This affords them the opportunity to contribute their unique gifts and skills.

Having a microboard is a win–win situation. Firstly, as a family you are strengthened by the team. Secondly, the team members are rewarded for their help by being a part of something amazing. Thirdly, everyone – including the person with disability – is rewarded with the gift of friendship.

CHAPTER 31

A Home of One's Own

*"There are only two ways to live your life. One is as though
nothing is a miracle. The other is as though everything is."*

— *Albert Einstein*

By the end of 2017 Greg and I were conscious of there
being only six months left on Emma's rental lease.
We talked about the possibility of Emma having a
permanent place of her own. She was clearly very happy in
the rental unit, but there would be benefits associated with
moving into a place of her own:

- She would be paying a similar amount of money to
  purchase her own place as she was paying in rent

- Her payments would eventually lead to
  ownership, which provides her with security

- She would have more choice and control over
  what she could do in a property

- She wouldn't have to pack up and move, which is always a risk when you are not the owner of a property
- We would feel peace of mind knowing that when we are gone Emma is happy and settled (if she continued to rent, at some point she would need to move – if this happened after we were gone, Roshan and Laksiri would have to find a suitable place for her)

One of Emma's clients is a real estate agent, so I contacted staff at the agency and provided a brief that listed our needs. Very quickly they had a place to show us; it was a lovely little two-bedroom duplex in a really quiet part of the city. As soon as I walked into the unit I knew that it was the one. We did look at other properties but this very first one had a beautiful feeling about it. I just knew this was the right place for Emma.

Then, there was the matter of talking to Emma about the move and why this was a good idea. To begin with she was understandably confused, because in her mind her current unit was "home". Back to the creative thinking. I showed her photos on her iPad of the downstairs room at our home where she had begun her independent living. I asked her, "Who owns this one?" She answered, "Mummy". Then I showed her photos of her rental and asked her the same question. She answered that she owned it. So I showed her the photo of the people who owned the property and ex-plained that she had been paying them money to live there, but it wasn't hers. Then I showed her photos of the new unit and explained that this one would be hers. We went back over this process a couple more times until she was clear that the new place would be hers.

The next step was to take her to see the new property. She was quite relaxed about going to look at it. As we wandered through the rooms we talked about where she would put her

TV and her DVDs. We looked at both bedrooms and I asked her which one she thought was the best one. We had a look outside so that she could see that she would now have an area we could make into a nice outdoor space for her.

I asked Emma's staff to make sure they drove past the new place each day with her. I also asked them to say, "Look, there is your new house!" and to talk to her about how exciting it was to be moving into her own place.

Because this property was a lot bigger than the rental, I suggested that she might like to get another lounge chair for her guests to sit on. I said that we could go and have a look for one, if she wanted to. Emma was very keen to choose a new lounge and a couple of footstools. I had no involvement in what she chose; in the end, they were three different colours. This was no problem because she likes lots of colour.

In July 2018 Emma moved into her own little home. We didn't unpack anything for her before she moved into the new place because I wanted her to have the experience of deciding where and how she wanted her home to be set up. So as I took things out of boxes I asked her where she wanted them. She would look around and tell me where she wanted them to go. I did the same with her bedroom – she knew exactly where she wanted her bed, and she told me to put the little tables on either side of the bed. Of course, this all took a long time. However, it was important that Emma not just understand that this was her own place, but that she could decide how she wanted to live in it. This would give her the experience of feeling ownership of, and control over, her home. My strategy paid off, and Emma smoothly settled into her new home – it felt as though she had always been there.

Emma has a strong sense of ownership of this property. Recently, Greg was explaining to her that he had made arrangements for a pest company to come in to spray for

Emma's very own home – it is her sanctuary

ants and cockroaches. He said that he would come over and let the man in while she was at work. Emma immediately told Greg very forcefully, "My home, not yours". Emma doesn't like anyone being in her home when she is not there.

As I write this, Emma's unit is having some renovation work done – namely, a deck to the side of her property, off the dining room. Our reasoning for building the deck is simple, but is once again based on the principles of SRV. The deck does a few things for Emma:

- It gives her more room, because the unit is small
- It provides another opportunity for Emma to entertain people
- It provides a way for Emma to express herself through decoration

When it comes to decoration, I want to share a little story with you – Emma had mentioned a couple of times that she wanted a picture of a tiger on the wall facing the deck, and on each occasion I was in a hurry and said, "Oh, yes, a tiger... we will have to look for a picture to put up out there". However, on another occasion she was determined to ensure that I *really* understood exactly what she meant. She took me by the hand to a wall where she has a lot of photos of her different holidays. In one of the photos she is standing beside a huge mural of a tiger at Melbourne's zoo. She signed to me, "The same out there", and I realised she didn't want a poster. She knew that she wanted a painting, and she found a creative way to show me that. Although Emma doesn't have a lot of spoken language, she is persistent about being understood. She also asked for the painting to be enormous, which is definitely not something I would have wanted for myself. But the point here is that it is *her* home, and if that is how she wants to express herself, then that's fine. She has started calling her home the "tiger house" (head to Emma's page on my website to see a video of her delighted reaction to the new mural: joannelynam.com/emma).

Not everyone thought that it was a good idea for Emma to move into her own place. One mother suggested to me that Emma would be at risk on her own. She said that she had placed her son in a group home so that he had company and staff to keep him safe. My response to this was that I wished them well. However, at same the time I was thinking that history reveals that all manner of abuses have occurred behind closed doors of places set aside to "keep people safe" – just as I have seen firsthand during my time working with the department.

I have met men who once lived in institutions, and while there had endured all kinds of horrific daily abuse. It was only when they were out of the institutions – and were provided with support to be able to communicate – that they could tell their stories of abuse. These stories spoke volumes about the lack of respect and care shown by their providers. I am in complete awe of people who have survived such abuse and have been able to forgive and move forward with their lives. While some of these survivors are not able to speak, communication programs on iPads have given them a way to be heard. Using this technology they have written some truly beautiful poetry. I am aware of one such man who, despite the abuse he suffered in an institution, has courageously gone on to create amazing paintings that bring joy to all who see them.

The idea that group homes are a way to keep people safe is a total fantasy. Having good connections with neighbours and friends, and a visible and valued role in the community, is what keeps *everyone* safe. We have all heard stories of an elderly person who died in their home and no one knew until a smell was noticed. How can that happen in societies that are wealthy and well resourced? It happens when people are not connected to their neighbours, and are not known and valued in their community. Having neighbours and work colleagues in Emma's life makes me feel that she is safe. Her life is lived in the light, not in the darkness behind closed doors.

I believe that a home is not just bricks and mortar. Our home is our sacred space, a place where we get to be ourselves. *Every* human being deserves to feel "at home".

CHAPTER 32

Stepping Up the Ladder of Independence

"Never surrender your hopes and dreams to the fateful limitations others have placed on their own lives."

— Anthon St Maarten

In 2018 Emma had another wonderful mini holiday. This time she wanted to see *Rocky Horror Show* in Melbourne, which would give her the opportunity to see a little of Melbourne, including Melbourne Zoo. As with previous holidays, the goal was for Emma to venture out into the world and explore it in a new way. *Rocky Horror Show* is Emma's favourite musical; she has it on DVD and watches it regularly. (For the 40th anniversary of the show, in 2019 a movie theatre here in Townsville held a *Rocky Horror* night. The theatre was decorated in keeping with the theme, and the staff dressed up. Emma was so excited about going to see it at the movies. She and her new staff member Zoe went as characters Columbia and Magenta and had a great night.)

August 2018 saw Emma given the opportunity to present her story at a conference in Townsville. When I was asked her whether or not she would like to share her story, I wasn't sure how she would feel about standing up in front of a large crowd. However, once again – what do I know? Emma very happily agreed to do the presentation. My friend Ann Greer was coordinating and supporting the three speakers who had disabilities. Prior to this, Emma had not taken a lot of notice of Ann. However, you may remember me mentioning in chapter 22 (in regards to Emma cooking at home) that when something or someone is relevant, Emma will take notice. Ann's presence in Emma's life now had a purpose and meaning – she wasn't just one of Mum's friends; she was someone who could help Emma with her presentation.

I was absolutely stunned by Emma's level of commitment to making this presentation. It was all created on her iPad, using the Pictello app. She really enjoyed scrolling through all of the photos on her iPad and choosing which ones she wanted to include in the presentation. In fact, while we were putting together the story there were a couple of photos that Emma wanted to use but I had forgotten to add them – however, she certainly hadn't forgotten. She made me stop while she slowly scrolled back through the photos until she found what she was looking for. This told me that Emma valued the experiences she had had and wanted to share them. She certainly didn't appreciate me overlooking even one of these moments. Once all of the information and pictures were uploaded, Emma had several practice runs of the presentation with some of her business clients. Then she got up early on the Saturday before to have a practice with Ann.

The timeslot for Emma and the other two presenters was 11am on a Tuesday, which was smack in the middle of her workday. I suggested that she could cancel the first client for the day so that she would have plenty of time to get to the venue for her presentation. No way – Emma wasn't going to cancel. She decided that she would get up two hours earlier and complete the work for that first client before the presentation.

On the morning of the conference she got up and got ready early. She did her first client's work and then headed to the conference. When Emma turned up with her support worker I could see that she was a bit anxious about the number of people in the hall. Once we got the iPad hooked up to the projector and speakers, Emma took her place and did the presentation, and thanked people for listening. She then kissed me goodbye and went straight back to work. I had hoped that she might stay and have lunch with me... how foolish of me. Having the opportunity to share her story of success and determination was an important milestone for her. It gave her the opportunity to see and hear the applause from a large audience. There is no better way to be validated than that.

You see, I had actually been the one asked to present Emma's story at the conference. However, I explained that it was Emma's story and therefore hers to tell, not mine. I knew that if she could overcome her anxiety it would be a wonderful life-affirming experience for her. Seeing people respond so well reinforced what I and many others had been telling her, that she was a successful young businesswoman. If I had done the presentation she wouldn't have had this value-adding experience.

In August 2019 we were preparing for Emma to go to New Zealand for a holiday when she was given an opportunity to present her story at a disability expo in Christchurch. Denise (who had replaced Raghu as one of Emma's support workers) travelled with Emma for this working holiday. It was wonderful to see the level of maturity in Emma compared to when she first travelled overseas in 2017. This time she

FaceTimed me, panning her phone around her hotel rooms to give me a view from her window and to share how lovely each room was. Denise captured some amazing moments of Emma presenting but also just enjoying herself, just like any 25-year-old. After Christchurch they flew to Auckland to take in more sights. Emma and Denise were very warmly welcomed to Auckland by a provider who had arranged for Emma to present her story to a group of families. This second invitation was only possible due to the support of Lorna Sullivan; she now lived back in New Zealand but even from across the Tasman she was still helping us.

I was keen for Emma to take up this opportunity, not only to explore and enjoy a different country and culture, but because it would be a working holiday. She would get to experience something that many young people of her age get to experience – the combination of travel and work. I also see that each time Emma attempts something new, it gives her the opportunity to take another step up the ladder towards greater confidence and independence. With each step up, she lets go of me just a little more.

CHAPTER 33

Getting Out of the Way

"Life is like a stage play. Some actors have big parts to play while others have no lines at all. Each part has a purpose; each part was written to be part of the bigger purpose of 'The Play of Life'."

— *Joanne Lynam*

There are a number of reasons why getting myself out of the way is essential for Emma to have a good life. It is important that she understands that she can work with, and grow from spending time with, other people. Staff come into Emma's life with their own history and life experiences, and that offers Emma a different lens through which to see the world. The staff approach Emma in very different ways than do we as her family, and this helps her to be flexible and more easily embrace change. If she only had the opportunity to work with and be with her family it would limit her and prevent her from becoming a strong and independent woman. Also, Greg and I are now in our 60s – we will not outlive Emma, so I see my life's work from here on as preparing her for when we are gone. While you might think it's sad, or morbid, that I say this, I don't see this at all. I feel blessed to have the opportunity every day to look into my own mortality. Looking at my future death is a great gift; it means I don't waste time on shit that doesn't matter. It has spurred me on to put things in place for Emma so that she can continue to grow long after I have gone. Yes, she will grieve and no doubt struggle, but I will have failed her if she feels she cannot go on without me.

As I mentioned earlier, Kylie and Emma had an instant connection. Kylie had a lovely inclusive way of working. It's really rare for any of us to find a person with whom we have an instant and magical connection. Kylie was responsible for many of the opportunities Emma had in exploring the fun of Townsville's nightlife. This might not seem important, but I felt (and still do feel) that young people with a disability often live the lives of their older parents. They are never given the chance to meet other young people of their own age or to explore and enjoy the world in the way that young people do. To just go out clubbing and have a wild night of fun. When we were younger many of us had nights such as those, and woke up the next morning a little worse for wear. The point here is that we had the opportunity to run free, off the chain of our daily commitments and responsibilities, and to dance the night away in the arms of someone we liked.

When Raghu first starting working with Emma, it offered her the gift of beginning to see herself outside of her role as daughter and sister. She now had the role of a boss. Raghu had a very respectful and sensitive way of working with her but he was also aware that he was, in fact, working in a business and that it needed to be treated like any other business. By this I mean that he had to support Emma in understanding the importance of honouring her commitments to the businesses at which she worked, and to conduct herself in a professional manner.

Emma in her home, cuddling her much-loved baby niece, Penny

Emma became very fond of Raghu and I knew that his departure from the role would be difficult for her – but it would also be good for her. Denise came into the role just as Raghu was leaving, and initially Emma was very cool towards her. Denise is remarkably patient and was able to sit within the uncomfortableness that Emma projected when she first started. Being able to just sit in an uncomfortable space and not be swept away by those feelings is a great gift. I have great admiration and respect for Denise's ability to just BE with Emma and not focus on the doing. When you are working with a person like Emma, who is sensitive to the feelings of those around her, just "being" is a great gift.

Then we have Zoe, who is quite a remarkable young woman for someone so young. She has a level of compassion and tolerance that is way beyond her years. When we began working with a speech pathologist who was introducing a whole new world of communication to Emma, I must say that I felt daunted by it and I think Emma did, too. While the speech pathologist had the systems to help Emma communicate better, someone needed to help her put the systems into action. Zoe was that someone. Watching Zoe not only grasp the concepts of SRV but be able to bring them to life is very gratifying. I feel very proud of Zoe.

Although I value the different perspectives and experiences that staff bring into Emma's life, I also feel that stability and consistency are important. Therefore, if I had been in control there would have been little to no change of staff in Emma's life. However, I am so glad that she has had a couple of challenging years with a lot of staff turnover. She has become so much more flexible and resilient by having to adjust to different people, and by having to assess their energy in different situations. It has also been a great lesson for me in trusting that the book of Emma's life was written long ago and that it is all unfolding at the right time, with the right people.

Emma is very clear about what she wants for her life and who she wants in it. At one stage I fired a particular staff member because I didn't think they were right for the position. But through her persistent reaching out to this person, Emma drew her back into her life. Emma made it very clear to me how she felt. She kept signing the person's name and telling me that she liked her. Emma was inviting her to afternoon tea on a regular basis. One day she pulled me over to some photos on her wall and pointed to this particular person's photo, signing, "I like that one". Later, when I asked Emma who she would like to take her to an upcoming movie, suggesting she choose someone from her three staff, Emma said, "No". She signed the name of the person I had fired and again pointed to her photo.

Once again, Emma was the teacher and I the student. How could I talk about self-determination and then override her choice? So this particular young person came back into Emma's life. On the evening on which they went out together, I realised that the lesson for me in this situation was to look differently! While I watched them get ready to go, all I saw were two beautiful young women off to have a fun night out. Emma's ability to pick up on and respond to the energy of others is something that I don't have, so I now trust that she sees beyond what I am able to see. The really interesting thing about this young woman is that she has a very good connection with Emma – I hadn't been able to see this previously. However, I suspect that Emma always had.

In order to respect Emma's desire to have this young person back in her life, I crafted a specific role for her whereby she was only doing social things with Emma. Recently, I sent this young woman off to SRV training and I was very pleasantly surprised to see her level of understanding of (and commitment to) its principles. With more time and training I feel that this young woman will be a great asset to Emma's team.

In the early part of 2019 Emma seemed somewhat distracted and disconnected. I spoke with her about how she was feeling and she said she was fine. I asked if she was happy with her work and her life and she again said she was fine. However, she still seemed to be drifting. So I asked Karen to do some work with her to see if she could get to the bottom of it.

After their session, Karen explained to me that she had tested Emma at all levels, and had checked on how she was feeling about the different areas of her life (namely, work, staff and home). Emma was happy with all of these areas. However, Karen told me that Emma had a deep longing within her. A longing to share her life with someone. Karen asked Emma if this also meant that this person would be sharing her home. To this, Emma said, "Yes". It would be someone with whom she could share the cooking and cleaning, and with whom she could watch DVDs. Karen explained that Emma longs for someone who would just "get" her, and with whom she can communicate on all levels.

As Emma's mum, this was both heartbreaking and reassuring to hear. I felt sad to think of Emma having such a strong longing within her that I didn't even know about. I also felt very happy and satisfied that Emma was expressing how much she loved her life, the life that she longs to share. I am enormously grateful to Karen for helping Emma give her inner feelings a voice. Karen had also spent some time talking to Emma about how powerful she was and that if she really wanted to have someone to share her life, she could draw that person to her. Karen has been working with Emma to help her understand that she can meditate on her desires and that this will bring those desires to her.

Recently, Emma was unwell with a virus. At the time, a much-liked staff member of hers was finishing work and moving town to take on a new role. I wondered if this might be playing a part in Emma's sudden decline in health. Karen reported to me that Emma was indeed sad and upset at the loss of this person from her life. She had indicated that she was tired of losing people. Karen showed Emma that each time a different person has come into her life she has grown from their energy and ideas, and they have grown from being with her. She showed her that she had also grown from the sadness that she experiences when each person leaves. Karen helped Emma to understand that this happens to everyone; we all feel sad when people we like leave our lives.

Emma recovered from the virus and quickly went back to work. The thing I was concerned about was whether Emma would be happy to work with the new staff member. I didn't need to worry – she embraced the new girl almost immediately. I am happy to say that they are working well together.

I cannot put a price on the enormous value and trust I place in the work Karen does with Emma. I am aware that Karen has done some work with other young people on the spectrum and that they, too, have benefited greatly from her support.

Without Karen's help I don't believe Emma would ever have become the Master Shredder. Yes, for sure I held a great vision for Emma of what her life could become. But it was Karen who helped her understand what that vision might look like. This meant that she could take those first steps on her journey to becoming the Master Shredder with Karen walking quietly, unseen, beside her.

I think back to the night on which I invited Karen and her husband to dinner, when Emma was doing her very best to ignore both of them. At the time, Karen mentioned that she didn't know much about Down syndrome or autism. As she took those early steps in working with Emma, she was unsure about the impact she could make. However, the sincerity of her desire to help Emma carried her across the wasteland of "not knowing" to the shores of real human connection. Karen has shared many times how the sessions with Emma were of enormous benefit to *her* – she gained as much from them as did Emma. Today, I look at the huge breadth of information and insight that Karen now has, particularly around autism, and I am in awe of the way she is *choosing* to make working with people on the spectrum her life's work.

If there is one thing that I hope families might take from this book, it is this: be open to receiving help, in whichever way it might show up in your life. Trust that no matter how it might appear, you have nothing to lose if you just take one step of courage.

CHAPTER 34

Seeing Perfection

*"What could you not accept, if you but knew that everything
that happens, all events, past, present and to come, are
gently planned by One whose only purpose is your good?"*

— *A Course in Miracles*

I believe that each of us comes to this earthly school
for a reason. We only need to attend the lessons that
we need to learn, such as forgiveness, compassion
or tolerance. There are no mistakes in life; everything is
happening at the right time for the right reason to the right
people. I have also come to know that there is a divine blueprint for our lives that lays out where we will go, who we will
meet and those people who become our family.

As a child growing up in Mt Isa I attended a local Catholic
primary school. Each year the school would be visited by
the "holy man". I have no idea if he actually was holy. We
just called him that because he travelled through western
Queensland with his van outfitted to sell holy goods; things

such as rosary beads and holy pictures. When I was about eight years old I (like all the other children at school) visited the van with my pocket money to see what I could buy. I clearly remember walking into his cramped little van and seeing a picture of a little black baby being watched over by a little black angel. I wasn't interested in anything else so I bought the picture. I remember thinking that there was something really special about it – it was almost as though it was magical.

However, when I showed my mother what I had bought, she yelled at me, "What did you buy that for? That was a waste of money!" But I didn't care. I liked it, so I put it on my duchess. Each afternoon I would come home to find that Mum had placed it face down. Then I went off to Brisbane to study music and forgot all about the picture until Greg and I were setting up the nursery while we waited for Roshan's adoption to go through. It turned out, my sister had packed up my things into boxes and these were still at Mum and Dad's home. So I asked Mum for the boxes, and there was the picture. I put it up in the nursery. While we were waiting to adopt Roshan I often sat in the nursery and held the little picture that had called to me so long ago. I still have that picture in my meditation room. I feel sure that, as a little girl of eight years old, I was drawn so strongly to the picture by an inner knowing of the two beautiful boys I would adopt in my future. It had been as though my 30-year-old self was giving my eight-year-old self a glimpse into the future.

I know that Emma is perfect for the role she is here to play. In the eyes of many, Emma appears to have many imperfections. But appearances are deceiving. Sure, she can't read or write, or for that matter say a great deal. So what? She doesn't need words; she communicates through her presence and her touch. Emma is not limited to using words, which can often be clumsy and inaccurate and, if used incorrectly, painful for the person on the receiving end. Words are nowhere near as powerful as feelings. Sometimes, hollow words are all that remain when our true feelings have been sacrificed on the altar of social norms.

On numerous occasions over the years I have experienced Emma's ability to pick up on other people's energy, including my own. I couldn't count the number of times I have been swayed by someone's charm or intellect and not been able to see the truth of the person behind the mask of lies. But, every time, Emma had seen through them the first time she met them. My ego wouldn't let me see, until the damage was done. I have had so many conversations with families who have shared that their son or daughter on the spectrum has the same ability.

Surely this is a gift to be shared? A gift that can be used to help others understand what they just can't see? Could it be that at this time on our planet, when we have more people than ever before being born with autism, there is a divine plan at work here? Right now, the earth is feeling the heavy burden of humankind while, at the same time, we have the arrival of all of these pure-energy beings who live in the shadows of our community. At best, they are seen as a mystery; at worst, not functional or valuable.

But what if this is all wrong? What if people on the spectrum are the answer to our prayers, but we are so caught in the trap of our intellects, and from bouncing around in a hall of mirrors and listening to the cacophony of our own voices, that we can't see and hear what is right in front of us?

When Emma first started working I used to find it really interesting that she would make a connection with certain staff members at her workplaces – sometimes this person was not the point of contact I had for that particular business. In the beginning I saw that her clients were doing something wonderful for Emma, by giving her an opportunity to serve. But, as time passed, I began to see that these relationships were, in fact, equal, with both parties giving and receiving. Emma is able to offer them something that they can't see. Perhaps she offers them a vision or insight into their own perfection, their own enough-ness?

There have been support staff of Emma's with whom I have struggled, for various reasons. In hindsight, I accept that the only real challenge was my fearful thinking. I felt that only I really knew how to be and work with Emma. This is not right. Everyone who comes to work with her finds their own way of being with her. Each of these relationships has been perfect for them both. Emma offers a vision of people's true selves, which is perhaps not the way they view themselves. Through her lack of words, her signing the same thing 40 times (because she is anxious or isn't sure that her communication has been understood), and her telling them that she loves them, she helps to heal them. To those who are open, she teaches the value in focusing on *being with her*, not *doing for her*. Slowing down enough to just *be* with someone is enormously powerful.

A little while ago someone I know showed me a video of her son with autism waiting so excitedly at the airport to meet a young man who had previously worked with him. To see the genuine joy and love they obviously felt for each other was so beautiful. The mum told me that this particular staff member had been in a dark place, and he had felt that working with her son had saved his life. I think that is a great gift. No amount of counselling or therapy can even come close to the kind of heartfelt healing that happened just by being with her son – all without the need for words.

Just suppose that you are the manager of a large corporation and you have to recruit a new team member. You are staring at a large pile of resumes, and you know that there will be a substantial amount of "horse shit" to wade through. Now, imagine if, on the day of the interviews, you have sitting beside you a young person on the spectrum who has an incredible ability to read people's energy. This person knows what people are really feeling, not necessarily what they are saying. Think about that for a moment. Wouldn't it be enormously helpful to have that person be able to indicate who was full of horse shit? This would save you from employing a person who might not fit within the organisation – or who, worse still, causes disharmony.

Although they seem to have a reduced ability to "communicate", some people on the spectrum are actually brilliant at this. They communicate not through words, but through their razor-sharp sensory perception. They feel what passes us by. I find that when I just sit and *be* with Emma there are no words needed; she will help me to feel what she feels. People with autism just love for love's sake, and to heal people, not to get something or to control someone. In some ways I see people with disability – particularly those on the spectrum – as superheroes because of their ability to pick up on what we don't notice.

When Emma was very little I mourned the fact that she wasn't able to hear – I saw it as a loss. I felt that she would miss out on so much by not being able to hear. I thought about all the beautiful poetry and music she would never hear, and I felt a loss. But the universe has a perfectly balanced set of scales for all of our lives. So, although I saw a lack of hearing, communication and intelligence, I didn't see initially that the universe had gifted Emma with a finely tuned sense of where and how to touch and heal. She did this not through some formal healing modality. She did this just by her sense of "knowing" and by drawing to her those who needed her and her particular way of being with them. Once they had received what they needed, they then moved out of her life. When I think back to my struggle at the time of the hearing loss diagnosis, I am now grateful for all of the painful words she has never had to hear. I wish that I, too, could have been spared the wounds of so many unkind words that I had the ability to hear.

People with an intellectual disability are quite uniquely placed to see things differently. Their apparent dis-ability is, in fact, a great ability because it affords them a way of looking at the world through an entirely different lens. They don't share the "must hurry, got to achieve things" way that we see the world. Where we see difference, they bring unity. Where we see sameness, they experience uniqueness. Where we see broken, they move to heal and rebuild. My experience of people with disability has also led me to see within them an incredible ability to forgive. To be able to drop a hurt in an instant and move on – unlike many of us, who often hold on and feed the hurt until it consumes us. Their willingness to open the door again and again, despite the way they have been treated. Their capacity to see joy in simply sharing your company – this is like salve on a wound. You did not know you needed the salve until it was given so freely and eased the pains you had no way to touch. Their heartfelt presence is here to serve at a time when, if we will just open our hearts, we will surely see that they are the answer to our prayers.

Many years ago, before Emma was in our lives, we were on holidays in Brisbane and I went to a workshop on "auras". The different colours of aura are meant to indicate various levels of love, understanding and openness. Someone asked the presenter if he had ever seen a golden aura. This is, if you like, the highest and the rarest kind of aura; it's rare because it is only around a person who embodies pure love. He answered that he had, in fact, seen a golden aura, but only once. He explained that he was in a shopping centre and up ahead of him was a mother pushing a stroller. Coming from the stroller was a golden aura. He said he walked quickly to get ahead of the mother, and when he looked back and into the stroller he saw that the baby had Down syndrome. I sometimes think back to hearing about this little baby with the golden aura and wonder how many lives the child had the opportunity to touch and heal, without anyone even knowing.

What if we truly embraced people with disability? What if we gave them meaningful roles that employed their unique skills to help us, instead of seeing them as not able to fit in or function? Imagine the golden-aura baby with Down syndrome having an opportunity to create a small healing practice for himself.

One day my friend Ann and I were having a coffee together and, as is usually the case, our conversation was focused on current issues within the disability sector. Ann has a daughter with Down syndrome, though her daughter is a lot older than Emma. Ann said something that stayed with me and really made me think. She said, "I thought I was standing on the edge of a revolution 20 years ago and here we are still dealing with the same thing". Her words stayed with me and I kept thinking about "standing on the edge of a revolution".

Eventually I asked the universe what I was meant to learn from these words. I looked up the word "revolution" in the dictionary, and it was defined as the violent overthrow of a social order or government. I then felt drawn to look up the word "evolution", and this was said to be a gradual move from simplicity to complexity, or an unfolding of events. As I sat with these words and their meanings, I considered that revolutions can rise up quickly and carry their supporters along. But many people get left behind or hurt by revolutions. Evolution is what is needed; not just for people on the fringes of our society, but for the good of the whole of society. We need to gradually raise the level of consciousness of the entire community so that we are all valued and viewed as equal.

Science is now showing us that we are not wired for division and conflict; rather, we are wired for cooperation. Scientists working with cells have seen this when cells are placed into a foreign environment. The cells don't fight each other. They cooperate to help each other. Division and conflict come from prejudice and fixed ideas, yet babies aren't born with these. They are open to exploring their world without judgement, just with wonder. We are stronger when we are together.

Over the years my spiritual journey has brought some amazing books into my life, books that have helped to shape who I am and to define what's important to me (you can find a list of these in the Resources section at the end of this book). I understand that each book came into my life only when I was ready for the journey that the book held. These books have helped me look beyond what I previously thought I KNEW to show me that anything is possible. I also know that I needed to read each of these books, meet different people, and have all the challenges that have come into my life. These challenges ranged from being raped, to dealing with bureaucrats in various departments to be able to adopt our two amazing sons, to the heartbreak of trying to craft a good life in the community for Emma at a time when the community didn't want to include people like her. I have had the good grace to get to know and be inspired by those who have walked the path before me and graciously shared their journey – people like Ann and the families and staff from CRU. They fought all of these battles long before me, and generously shared what their journey taught them. This was all so that the tiny seed lying dormant within me could awaken and grow to become the book that you are reading. And it's no accident that you have chosen to pick up this book and read it.

I find it fascinating that right now on our planet we have, on the one hand, a great deal of unrest in many parts of the world – in our political systems, banking systems and the challenges happening within the natural world. On the other hand, we have some amazing teachers talking about working with energy (and, basically, everything is energy). People like Dr Joe Dispenza, Gregg Braden and Dr Bruce Lipton, each in their own way helping to elevate the consciousness

And it's no accident that you have chosen to pick up this book and read it.

of thousands of people across the globe so that we can make the huge changes needed for what lies ahead. These changes and challenges will not be solved by using our old ways of thinking and being. We will need a much higher level of consciousness to navigate our way as our old systems fail. Surely we will need everyone's gifts to make this shift.

The connectedness of things in the world and our universe has always fascinated me – it is all connected in many ways. The way the tides are influenced by the moon. The way a group of young women living together will eventually all menstruate at the same time. The way our body's blood pressure is very similar to the way a tree draws up nutrients from the ground. The way birds know when to fly south for the winter. The way a caterpillar slowly undergoes a great metamorphosis and emerges as a butterfly. The way a tiny cluster of cells inside the womb eventually emerges as a baby.

Scientists use animals to test new drugs before giving them to humans. Why is this so? Because despite the outward appearance of these animals, we share a great deal of DNA with them. I love the way the life of a forest is so perfectly ordered and balanced, with some species of plants adapted for living in the shadows and others only surviving at the top of the forest in full sun. Some animals eat birds, birds eat insects and insects eat plants, all living in perfect harmony. Even when a tree comes to the end of its life and falls to the forest floor it is still working in harmony. It does this by providing a place for small creatures to live and food for termites and other insects. As all of these creatures and plants die, their decaying bodies provide more nutrients for the forest's soil – every leaf that falls from a tree to the floor has a further purpose. It's all divinely crafted, down to the tiniest detail.

If we look at the human species for a moment... why would there be no divine purpose for this species? Of course there is – the divine energy that beats in the heart of every creature in the bush or forest beats in the heart of every human. There is also a divine plan for each person. But each person has free will and a divinely given intellect, so while the script may be written for our lives we all have the choice to accept the script, or not.

The human species is responsible for the destruction of large parts of the natural world, and the impact that this has had on other species. Sadly, for the most part we have lost our connection with the natural world, with large parts of the human population now living in mega-cities. We all have the same divine light within us, but we spend most of our lives covering it with the illusionary lampshades of life; namely, the lampshade of our "stuff" or our jobs and our position in life. That divine light is always there, whether or not we know it.

About 10 years ago I read a beautiful book by Dr David Hawkins entitled *Power vs Force*. In this he described his research into consciousness and how he used behavioural kinesiology (muscle testing) as a tool that would provide truthful answers. His testing was repeated numerous times across the globe with people from diverse cultural backgrounds. The results of these tests consistently offered the same results. He ultimately developed a way of "calibrating" human emotions, and ranked the quality of the emotions by number. His work shows us the benefits everyone enjoys when we raise the consciousness of a group, city or country.

Wouldn't it be amazing if, instead of governments fighting it out in parliament over a piece of legislation, they just quietly sat and used kinesiology to determine if the legislation they had drafted was strong or weak? This same test could be applied to social policies that are put forward, to determine whether or not they are weak. Before people were elected, wouldn't it be helpful to find out where their energy level was sitting? Surely a leader with a higher level of consciousness would be of greater service than one with a lower level? What if schoolchildren learned kinesiology and how to apply it? It could be used to test whether or not particular subjects were worthwhile for individual students.

Looking beyond the classroom, it could be applied in medicine to test whether or not a particular medication is going to be useful for a patient. In the mental health field, it could be used to help doctors determine the best treatment for their patient. For the parents of a child with a disability, it would be very helpful to first calibrate the energy level of any prospective provider, and to determine the conscious-ness level of the organisation. Imagine knowing the energy level of a potential provider!

Dr Wayne Dyer is another writer whose profound work has played a big part in my journey towards understanding. I couldn't count the number of times I have retreated from the world and into the loving embrace of one of his books. I had the great good fortune to attend his final Melbourne workshop in 2015. I recall walking away from the workshop with an overwhelming sense of sadness. As I walked back to my hotel I tried to comfort myself with the thought that, perhaps, I might get to the US to see him on stage again or attend another of his workshops. But something told me that I would never see him again. He died about a week later. I still draw great comfort from his books. In some cases I may be reading a book of his for the second or third time but something new is always revealed to me.

A few years ago I read Dr Dyer's book *The Power of Intention*, in which he shares a wonderful story of a boy with a disability who attended a local special school. I'll share the story here in my own words, and I will call the boy William.

One afternoon William and his dad were walking home from school. As they neared a park where a group of boys were playing baseball, William mentioned that he would like to play. William's dad asked one of the boys if his son could join them. "Sure", he said. William waited for his turn to bat – and, remarkably, the boys of both teams seemed to silently agree to look after William. They pitched slow balls that were easy for him to hit. They did this so that a boy who could barely run and had never held a bat could have the opportunity to be included, to be part of a team. At first glance it might seem as though one team of boys were destined to lose their game by agreeing to send William in to bat. However, William gave both teams a gift. He gave them the gift of seeing beyond just winning a game – instead, they were able to see the greater purpose of "the game of life".

I really love this little story because it shows us that just by being who he was, William gave the boys playing baseball a great gift. He gave them an opportunity to raise their consciousness to a much higher level. I am sure those boys all went home feeling a far greater sense of satisfaction and purpose than if they had won the game.

The Weave of Life

Woven into the cloth of the ordinary
shines luminous the strand of the extraordinary.
This fabric emblazoned with colours of hue,
sometimes looks old, sometimes looks new.
Often the luminous is not seen in the thread,
but there on the loom of mankind it is spread.
So many frayed edges hemmed together,
holding strong in many a weather.

The miraculous weave of the dull and the grand,
perfectly woven together, strand by strand.
On the loom thin strands of anguish and pain,
brought together with patience and love, not disdain.
A golden thread tinged with the tragic,
conceals the moment of its own magic.
It is not given by metre of measure,
silence the key to unlock its treasure.
Some say it is given to a chosen few,
but none are chosen – the miracle is you.

Joanne Lynam, 2018

CHAPTER 35

And So It Is

"Don't be fooled by what you think you see.
If you think you see a person with a disability,
look again, look again, for you see nothing."

— *Joanne Lynam*

While you have been reading this book you may have noticed the importance that "purpose" has played in my life. At some point in all of our lives, we wonder about our purpose. We ask, "Am I living my true purpose? What is my purpose? Why am I here?" For a long time I had these thoughts and read a small library of self-help books on the topic of finding purpose. I did work-shops and listened to teachers talk about "one's purpose in life". Ultimately, what I have come to understand is that each of us comes to this earth with our own blueprint. This includes when and where we will be born, who will be our parents, who will be our partners and children, and all of our major life events and challenges.

I believe that I simply needed to live through the experiences of my life to understand the purpose that was held within it. The concept of "resilience" has been key for me in the realisation of my purpose. As I've mentioned previously, I eventually came to see that the purpose of the rape was so that I might become aware of my own resilience and to understand that I am not defined by one moment in time. Then, by being aware of my resilience I was able to hang on through the difficulties of Laksiri's adoption and bring him into our family. Also, I knew there was a reason why I had been shown that I was having a baby with Down syndrome – there was a purpose, and part of that was the chance to deepen my resilience (I've observed that resilience is common in many, many mothers who have given birth to magnificent souls who happen to have Down syndrome).

Purpose isn't the destination; it's the journey. Consider a person whose greatest wish is to be at the top of their game – to be recognised, respected and financially rewarded. However, when they achieve their goal and are at the very top, they often feel a longing for all of the work, challenges and striving it took to get them to the top. They feel they have lost their sense of purpose.

Some time ago I was at a large conference that focused on ways to think about people with disability being in work. I was with a group of families who were all very enthusiastically sharing stories about their family member who had a disability. I felt a lovely feeling of love wash over me. I am not sure exactly who or what I felt this love for and it didn't really matter. In that moment I was no longer standing talking with this group; instead, I felt as though I was now hovering above the whole conference, and then the whole building, the whole city, the whole country and the entire earth was below me. In that brief moment I had an insight into the perfection of the way we all come to this earth with everything that we need to fulfil our purpose.

Emma's purpose was always there in her desire to be independent. It was also there in her inability to read and write and in her ability to sit for long periods of time and do something that – to others – would seem to be a mindless, repetitive job. For her, it was calming.

I saw that my purpose had always been clearly visible on the loom of my life. A hint of this had been given to me so many years ago in the ashram, when I heard the swami explaining to a group of people that the way to enlightenment was just as sound for one who served their family. My purpose was woven into my role as a mum. My purpose was always there, even as a young girl in my love of poetry and words and in my ability and willingness to speak up. Emma arriving in my life just brought it all together.

I also saw that each of these beautiful families with whom I was speaking had something in common. Each parent was linked by a golden thread to their purpose and to the purpose of their child.

This understanding seemed to happen in an instant – the next second I was back at the conference with the group of families, listening to them sharing stories about their loved one who had a disability. In that moment I could see the purpose for each person. The thing that so often seems like a roadblock, or a problem, is part of the purpose – right there, hiding out in the open.

I was brushing my teeth the other night, and out of the blue a beautiful analogy came to me about our purpose:

A human life is a little like a string of pearls.

However, we never notice the string quietly holding it all together.

Without the string the pearls would just be rolling aimlessly around.

Our purpose is like the string holding the pearls in place.

We don't see this purpose, which brings all the different parts of a person's life together.

We only see the beauty and value of a life – what the person does, where they live and who they live with.

When a person is living their purpose, they shine like luminescent pearls held together by an unseen string.

So, having shared all of this with you, I am now asking you to sit quietly and consider what is the purpose for your loved one (or the person with whom you work) who has a disability. Also consider how your purpose is woven with theirs. This may be the one reason why you were drawn to this book – to realise your divinity and the perfection of life.

CHAPTER 36

My Purpose Finds Its Home

"We shall not cease from exploration, and the end of all our exploring will be to arrive where we started and know the place for the first time."

— TS Eliot

I never ever imagined that I would write a book. In fact, I was probably the person who would say, "No, I don't have any desire to write a book – that's not for me". I am also pretty sure that my teachers would have agreed that I most certainly would *not* be the student to go on to write a book. But here I am.

As I've mentioned earlier, the title for this book was given to me many years ago in the form of a poem, just after Emma was born. In 2018, I had a dream in which I was writing a book, although it wasn't clear to me what I was writing about. When I woke I thought, "I wonder what that means? Obviously it doesn't mean that I will write a book". A few months later I had the same dream. Again, I thought little of it – only that it must have some other meaning for me. Then, in May 2019, I had the same dream yet again.

Later that morning, as I checked my emails, I saw an email from a site from which I often purchased books. I scrolled through the email and came to a large red button that asked the question, "Is there a book in you?" For some reason, I clicked on the button. It asked for some contact information, so I entered this and closed the computer. The next day I got a call from the publishing house, and the person asked me what I thought I might write about. It was the most bizarre experience – I just began describing this book to the person on the other end of the phone. Inside my head I was scream-ing, "Shut up, don't say that!" as I poured out the story that you have just read. Then I heard myself say something really terrifying. I said, "Yes, I think I can write this book".

Part of my purpose has always been to write this book, even though I have spent most of my life being very clear that oth-er, smart, people wrote books. Not me. Definitely not me.

Writing this book has been a challenge and a blessing. Looking back at painful situations from the past has given me the opportunity to see them now through the lens of hindsight, to see that those situations and people no longer hold any power over me. I am now able to see that they only seemed to have power over me because my experience at the time was of power-less-ness.

I'd like to share with you a listing of what, I believe, are the key points you could take away from this book:

1. Be bold. Dream big. Don't follow the herd.

2. Gather support around you. It doesn't have to be a microboard, but ask yourself this question:

if it takes a village to raise a child, what does it take to raise a child with a disability? The more people you have on your team, the more ideas and possibilities you will have available to you. Remember the analogy about a large roof-span needing a lot of support pillars to hold it up?

3. Be open to accepting help wherever and however it shows up. Even if it looks and sounds a bit weird. For example, earlier in this book I shared how much Emma benefited from the energy work that my friend Karen did with her. On the surface, it may have seemed strange to try something often considered to be outside the mainstream. But I am so grateful for the direction in which Karen's generosity and wisdom took us.

4. Look for groups and organisations that share a common dream of helping people with disability to live a good life

5. Consider the value of "roles" for a person with disability, instead of focusing on "busyness"

6. Reflect on what is thought of as "typical" for people of the same age as your child (taking into account what other people might be doing with their lives) and ensure that you frame possibility from that perspective

7. Be mindful of "image" – how do actions and outward appearances come across to someone who does not know that your child or client has a disability? Are they dressed in a way that means they look incapable, or are they acting in a way that might been seen as "childlike"?

8. Believe in the power of possibility – it will visit you with its amazing gifts

It is my hope that this book makes its way into the hands of families who are looking for a way forward for their loved one. I hope it helps providers to "look beyond what they think they see", and I also hope this book lands in the hands of people with a disability. Ultimately, I would like this book to act as a road map, offering people with disability a way to navigate their journey to a good life – a life in which they are empowered to choose what is right for them. I hope that, having read this book, you now feel the power of possibility lying quietly within you.

If you are reading this as the parent of a person with a disability, you are like me – you, too, accepted the contract offered to you so long ago. Sometimes this contract can feel very heavy. I have felt that heaviness myself. Please know that I am here for you. I have provided a list of resources after this chapter, and remember also that you can download the *Planning for Success* manifesto and affirmations at joannelynam.com/book-gift – these will give you extra support on your journey. If you have any questions about my story or you just need a little help to see beyond what is in front of you, please connect with me through the website. I would be honoured to be part of your support network.

Resources

It can be difficult to sift through all the information about providers and the supports that are available. Here are some resources that I hope help you to find your way through all the false promises and BS so that your loved one can get the kind of support they need to help them have a good life.

BOOKS THAT CHANGED MY LIFE

Autobiography of a Yogi by Paramhansa Yogananda

Dying to Be Me by Anita Moorjani

The Last Hours of Ancient Sunlight by Thom Hartmann

The Power of Intention by Dr Wayne Dyer

Power vs Force by Dr David Hawkins

The Secret Life of Plants by Peter Tompkins & Christopher Bird

Truths Among Us by Derrick Jensen (ed)

You Are the Placebo by Dr Joe Dispenza

BOOKS THAT CHANGED MY THINKING ABOUT DISABILITY

Letting in the Light by Michael Kendrick

Our Presence Has Roots by Janet Klees

The Shouted Goodbye by Jeremy Ward

We Come Bearing Gifts by Janet Klees

ORGANISATIONS THAT HAVE INSPIRED ME

Community Connections Australia – communityconnection.org.au

Community Resource Unit Ltd (CRU) – cru.org.au

Imagine More – imaginemore.org.au

Inclusion Solutions – inclusionsolutions.org.au

Microboards Australia – microboard.org.au

Towards Better – towardsbetter.com.au

SOCIAL ROLE VALORISATION (SRV) EXPERTS & ORGANI-SATIONS I RECOMMEND

Australian Social Role Valorisation Association – asrva.org.au

Jane Sherwin Consulting – sherwinconsulting.com.au

John Armstrong – johnarmstrong781c@gmail.com

Values in Action Association – viaa.org.au

Thanks

I would like to thank...

My husband Greg, for his patience and support throughout this book project, including all the hours he spent proofreading my writing.

My beautiful children, for choosing me as their mother. Roshan, thank you for the gift of your artwork in this book. Laksiri, you have been my greatest teacher – your resilience and gentle wisdom go way beyond your years. Finally, thank you, Emma. Your courage to choose to come into this life with so many challenges and yet not be defeated is the source of my passion and drive.

My dear friend Karen, for her friendship, kindness and support, and for being Emma's constant unseen champion.

Ann Greer, for the vision you held long before we entered this arena. For your courage to persist when all around you shouted, "Desist".

Lorna Sullivan, for your kind and encouraging hand as Emma and I took our first steps on the road to a good life.

The Community Resource Unit (CRU) – thank you for helping me dare to dream big.

Natasha Buttler, from Boost Marketing Services, for your great sense of humour (which you needed because of my lack of marketing knowledge!), your understanding of the importance and value of this book, and your commitment to getting it to the market.

Joanne Newell from Rich Life by Design – I brought you my diamond in the rough, but it was your care and understanding that crafted it into a beautiful book.

Thank you also to Amy De Wolfe. You took my "rough" ideas and applied your insight and sensitivity so that the intention of my book is clear and beautifully presented on each page.

I would also like to acknowledge and thank the local businesses that have supported Emma in her quest for a life of her own. I played a small part in Emma's story by being open to the idea of a business when it was shown to me in meditation, but the credit for Emma's success must go to the owners of local businesses who stood up with open minds and willing hearts and gave Emma an opportunity to show what she could do. Despite Emma sometimes being a bit withdrawn in the early days, they have continued to support her. I am incredibly grateful to all of these businesses for supporting Emma; she would be nowhere without them.

I would like to say a big heartfelt thanks to Dave and Adele from the farm for taking the shredder paper and putting it to such good use.

I spoke earlier of the connectedness of life. This is very much how we feel about each of these businesses – they are like an extension of our family. So whenever we need anything that their businesses provide, we support them by taking our business to them. If you live in Townsville, I highly recommend that you do the same:

Acacia Kitchens

Advanced Health and Hand Therapy

Assist Community Services

Bidfood

C & B Designs

Cleon Legal & Mediation Services

Colliers International Townsville

Community Gro

Core Developments NQ

Department of Transport and Main Roads

The Diabetic GP Clinic

Electro Train

Enhanced Health Therapy Service

Explore Property Townsville

Get Set Safety & Emergency Training

Green Light Home Loans

Higgins Coatings

Kent Removals & Storage

KLP Family Law

Langtree Consulting

Legalsense NQ

Lex Electrix

Mackey Wales Law

Markwell Group

My Foot Dr

Oar and Horan Dentists

Purcell Taylor Lawyers

Queensland Country Bank

Queensland Lower Limb Clinic

Queensland Youth Services

Ruhl Family Law Centre

Share House Youth Programs Inc

Skinworx

SLR Consulting

Steel Pacific Insurance Brokers

Steps Employment Solutions

Tardiss

Total Lifestyle Chiropractic

Travel Associates

The Ville

Yumba-Meta Limited

Reader, I thank you, too. Thank you for caring deeply about the person in your life who has a disability. Thank you for being their advocate. Thank you for exploring solutions and searching for inspiration. Thank you for reading this book.

About Joanne

Joanne Lynam believes in miracles. She also believes that every challenge that has come into her life has not been by accident – there has been a divine purpose for each and every one.

In the 1980s Joanne and her husband Greg adopted sons Roshan and Laksiri from Sri Lanka, and in 1994 Joanne gave birth to a daughter, Emma (who was born with disability).

It is through her children that Joanne's eyes were opened to society's blindness and bigotry, and to a strength that she hadn't ever realised she possessed.

Although she is now a social justice warrior, Joanne has been a life-long listener and seeker. She has worked within Queensland's justice department, and has seen firsthand the way that society devalues anyone who doesn't fit "the norm".

She knows that it is her life's work to advocate for the voiceless, and to help them reach their potential.

When Joanne isn't passionately advocating for change, she loves nothing more than being with her family, diving into a curry, savouring an icy cold kombucha, reading books (uninterrupted!) and strolling along Townsville's beautiful beaches.

To discover more about Joanne and how you can help to empower people with disability, head to joannelynam.com.

SPEAKING UP

for change

As a result of speaking up for her daughter Emma, Joanne has found herself speaking on many stages.

It's there that she shares her story of helping Emma to live to her potential. She also shares her practical solutions for effecting societal change and for helping "invisible" people to become noticed and valued.

With a refreshing blend of feistiness, compassion and wry humour, Joanne captivates audiences and inspires them to take real-world action.

TO BOOK JOANNE TO SPEAK AT YOUR NEXT ONLINE OR OFFLINE EVENT, HEAD TO:

joannelynam.com/media-speaking

Review Request

Dear Reader

If my book has struck a chord with you, I would love to hear what it was that resonated with you.

I would really appreciate it if you could share your thoughts by leaving a review.

To do this, simply go to the review section on the Amazon page for *An Angel at My Door.* Click on the big button that says "Write a customer review" and enter your star rating and written review.

Thank you so much...

Joanne

PS I would love to see you enjoying this book – please share a photo of yourself (and possibly even your loved one who has a disability) with the book on Facebook, and tag me by using @JoanneLynamSpeaker.